Understanding Cookery

Leisure Learning Series

Pottery and Ceramics
Roger Bunn

Woodworking
A. B. Emary

Understanding Cookery
Jenny Kavarana

Jewellery
David Marsh

Understanding Your Car
John Watson

Understanding Cookery

Jenny Kavarana

M

First published 1979 by
THE MACMILLAN PRESS LTD
London and Basingstoke
Associated companies in Delhi Dublin
Hong Kong Johannesburg Lagos Melbourne
New York Singapore and Tokyo

Typeset in 10/11 Century by
Illustrated Arts
and printed in Great Britain by
A. Wheaton & Co. Ltd.
Exeter

British Library Cataloguing in Publication Data

Kavarana, Jenny
Understanding cookery.— (Leisure learning).
1. Cookery
I. Title II Series
641.5 TX717

ISBN 0–333–27125–4
ISBN 0–333–23677–7 Pbk

Contents

Preface

How often have you read a recipe and at the end still not really known how to do it or understood the reason for doing it that way? For example, do you know why you should cook green vegetables in an uncovered pan or why a custard should be baked in a water bath? Do you know the reason for allowing certain pastries to relax before rolling them out or what you have done when your pastry comes out hard? Do you know how and why you *seal* meat or *flambé* a *sautéed* dish?

The distinguishing angle from which this book is written is that I normally teach cookery rather than write professionally about it. It is through cooking with a huge number of different people that culinary mistakes and misunderstandings can be anticipated and therefore prevented. It is impossible to ignore or forget the things that cooks who do not teach take as read. I remember an occasion many years ago when I first started teaching in London taking a class of students which included two men, both absolute beginners. At that time I assumed that *everyone* knew how to soften mushrooms and I assumed that everyone knew that green peppers have seeds in them which have to be removed before peppers are chopped. I later discovered that one man was seen rubbing the cap of each mushroom with a little lump of butter . . . and you can imagine how long it took to separate hundreds of seeds from the pepper after it had already been chopped! Of all the people I meet in the kitchen, it is the men who very often have had no previous cooking experience when they come to learn; they have not even watched cookery going on as girls do in their mothers' kitchens. It is students like these, who start learning from scratch, who are so often the most successful with regard to the dishes they produce, because they have to listen carefully to what is told to them and follow closely what to do in order to achieve any results at all—they have nothing else to go on. It has recently dawned on me why an absolute beginner can be successful in this way—it is learning good practice from the start and not allowing bad habits to develop. It is understanding the reasons for doing things.

My intention in writing this book is that you should use it in conjunction with the cookery books you already have—it is not meant as a recipe book as such. When your other cookery books fail to explain a point or do not give sufficient background information it is these explanations and this information you may find here.

If at this stage you are a beginner and clinging to the book you will find that eventually your cooking will become freer in style and you will gather, quite rightly, that some recipes are only meant as a guide in that the ingredients and the method by which they are used may be altered.

JENNY KAVARANA

The author wishes to make due acknowledgement to S. R. Pinks.

1

Batterie de Cuisine

The items that should be at the top of everyone's personal list of necessary kitchen equipment are knives, a wooden chopping board and pans. This applies however little a person cooks or likes cooking or whatever interest they have in it. Equally important is to recognise the right knife, the right board and good pans from the wide selection available in the shops, for this is the day-to-day equipment that is most frequently used. A bad choice will lead to real frustration — besides which, it is a pleasure to use the ideal tool for what-ever job is in hand. To give a few examples: a chopping knife must have a curved blade that will rock on its edge from the point to the heel — impossible with a straight edge; a chopping board should be of wood, which is, in comparison with the alternative, Formica, soft and quiet. Formica is slippery, squeaky and completely resistant to the knife which as a result will blunt more quickly anyway. A saucepan must be well balanced: it is no good and is dangerous if it keeps falling over because the handle is too heavy in relation to the base. Apart from this, the base of any pan should be reasonably heavy so that foods cook evenly in it and do not burn as they would in a pan with a thin base.

To recognise well-designed equipment made of good quality materials and then to meet the initial cost outlay is in the cook's own long-term interests. Generally speaking, worthwhile utensils and equipment are not pretty but are sturdy. Kitchen spoons should be made of all stainless steel and should have long handles, not glazed wooden handles that chip or coloured plastic ones that melt or loosen if accidentally left over the heat. In a practical kitchen you will not find novelty saucepans made of heat-resistant glass which crack with a single careless slip of the hand or those with a thin coating of printed coloured enamel which eventually chip and then so easily rust. Pans should be of heavy iron, copper, stainless steel, thickly enamelled cast iron or a combination of two of these metals giving the advantages of both. No one metal, however good, will suit all requirements — there must be a compromise. Copper, for instance, conducts heat well but is difficult to keep clean, yet stainless steel which is not affected by acids and is easy to maintain does not have the cooking qualities of copper.

One's choice is also affected by one's interests. Some people like to make pâtés and terrines and will collect a range of pottery terrines, tinned raised pie-moulds and other stoneware jars for potted meats while for another person cake icing and decorating might represent a lifetime's interest and these two cooks will have completely different sets of tools and equipment, in addition to the basic range. It is possibly best to make do with as little equipment as possible or at least to recognise before you buy it the really useful gadget compared with the novelty one. Some tools can be made to do more than the obvious job for which they were originally intended. A knife can be used for other jobs besides cutting and chopping, for example to mash garlic, thus making a separate garlic press unnecessary. A fork can be used instead of a lemon squeezer to extract juice from a lemon and the cook should also be able to separate the yolk from the white of an egg without the aid of yet another gadget. Combined together they make more washing-up and require storage space. Try not to buy too many gadgets.

One sure way of finding out which is the best equipment is to observe what the professional chefs use; alternatively, visit a catering equipment suppliers or ask for their illustrated catalogue. Such places include William Page of Shaftesbury Avenue and Jaeggi & Sons of Dean Street, both in London W1. Also in London, good domestic equipment and imported French cookware are to be found at Elizabeth David's shop in Bourne Street, at David Mellor in Sloane Square and at Divertimenti in Marylebone High Street. The ordinary high street alternative is a good hardware shop or the kitchen department of a large store.

Illustrations and further points on some important items

of kitchen equipment are given below.

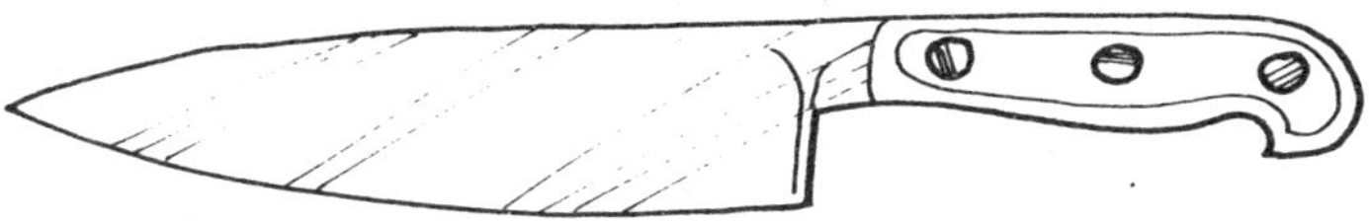

Figure 1.1 A French or chef's knife

The French or chef's knife (figure 1.1) is the most important knife in the kitchen. Choose an 18 cm (7 in.) blade in carbon steel. It is easy to keep a good edge on a carbon steel knife, whereas stainless steel is very hard and therefore difficult to sharpen. A French knife has a curved blade that rocks from the point as you chop. Examine the knife you are buying to see that the edge comes into contact with the board from the tip to the heel when stood up on its edge. If there are any gaps then food between these gaps will not get chopped. Buy a good quality knife, for example Sabatier, which will, of course, not be cheap. The balance of the knife is important and should feel heavy; it is less tiring than using a flimsy knife. You will observe that the blade continues right down into the handle and is riveted into the handle. As you hold the knife there is also room for your knuckles between the handle and the table as you chop. For the correct way to chop see p. 76. It is important to sharpen the knife correctly with a steel: see figure 1.2. You should draw the blade on its side across the steel, starting at the heel of the knife. Failure to observe this point results in a ruined knife, as shown in figure 1.3. This also applies when using a knife-sharpener which is not a steel.

There are various ways to sharpen a knife: in any event, sharpening must begin at the heel end of the blade, not at any distance down it. Failure to observe this point results in a notch being formed and it is easy to see that vegetables will not get chopped properly under this notch (see figure 1.3). Two safe ways are illustrated. In figure 1.2 *a* the steel is held point down on a table top to steady it. The knife is drawn across the steel from the heel to the point with the

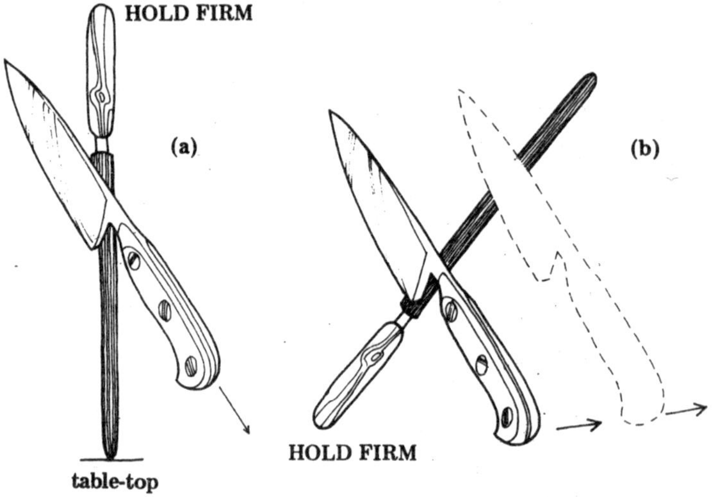

Figure 1.2 How to sharpen a knife

edge leading. You do this once in front of the steel then once behind it, repeating this action until you have a sharp edge. Another method, figure 1.2*b*, is to hold the steel crossways in front of you and to draw the knife across it from the heel to the tip with the edge trailing. You do this once on top of the steel then once underneath it, repeating this action until you have a fine edge. Whichever method is used, the knife should almost be lying on its side. It is considered correct, however, to sharpen a knife with the edge leading. Watch how a butcher sharpens his knife, but note that a butcher's knife is not meant for chopping onions, so it is not vital for him to keep the even curved edge of a French or a chef's knife.

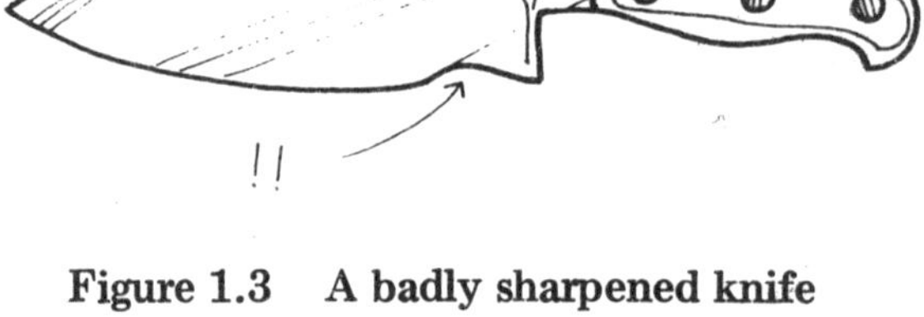

Figure 1.3 A badly sharpened knife

When once a fault such as that shown in figure 1.3 is allowed to develop, it only seems to get worse. The knife needs regrinding. See figure 1.2 for how to sharpen a knife.

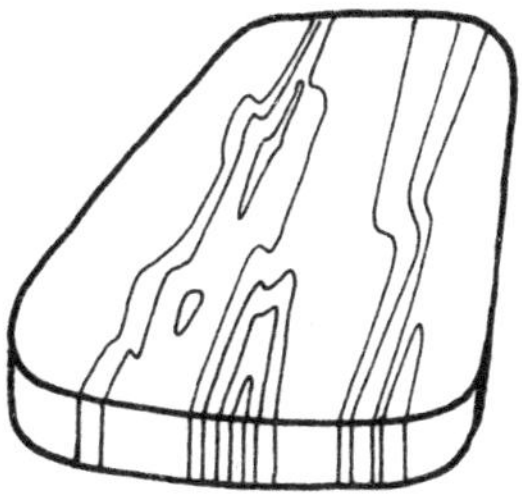

Figure 1.4 A wooden chopping board

A chopping board (figure 1.4) should be thick, about 2 cm, and the wood should be well seasoned so that it will not warp. A twisted chopping board is useless for chopping on. The wood should be in one piece; if there are joins in the wood they harbour bacteria. Some chopping boards have a shallow trough near the edge, which is useful for catching juices. If one side of the board looks different from the other, you could keep one for garlic and onions and the other for preparing fruits and other sweet dishes.

Figure 1.5 A serrated-edge knife

I find that a stainless steel serrated-edge knife such as the one made by Prestige (figure 1.5) is useful to have; it does not discolour fruits and vegetables required fresh in salads as a carbon-steel knife does. It is especially good for slicing tomatoes and removing the skin and pith from oranges when these are required in a dessert.

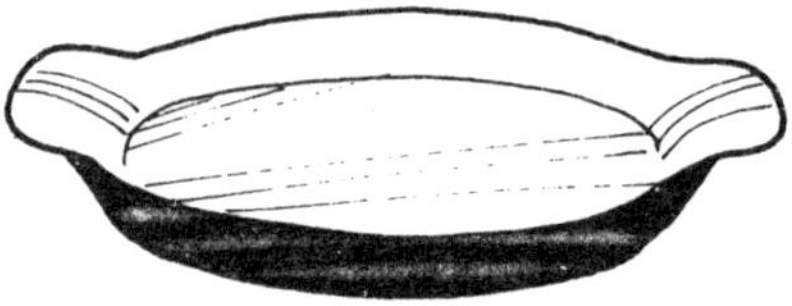

Figure 1.6 A gratin dish

An enamelled cast iron dish (figure 1.6) can be used on top of the fire as well as in the oven; however, they are usually made of ceramics. Lug-handles at either end facilitate removal from a hot grill or oven.

Figure 1.7 A deep casserole

A deep pot with a wide belly and a narrower neck (figure 1.7) is good for all-round cooking and cuts down the loss of moisture from the food through evaporation. A wide, shallow casserole on the other hand can double as a gratin dish. The lids of all casseroles should fit well.

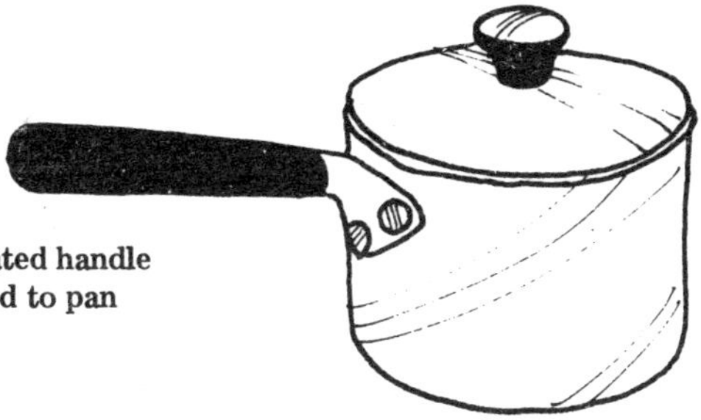

Figure 1.8 A good saucepan

No one metal suits all requirements—it is possibly a good idea to have a selection of metals. In any event, choose a saucepan that has a heavy base: this ensures even cooking and also helps prevent burning. The lid should fit tightly—a loose lid encourages evaporation. The handle should be insulated and should be riveted to the pan (figure 1.8).

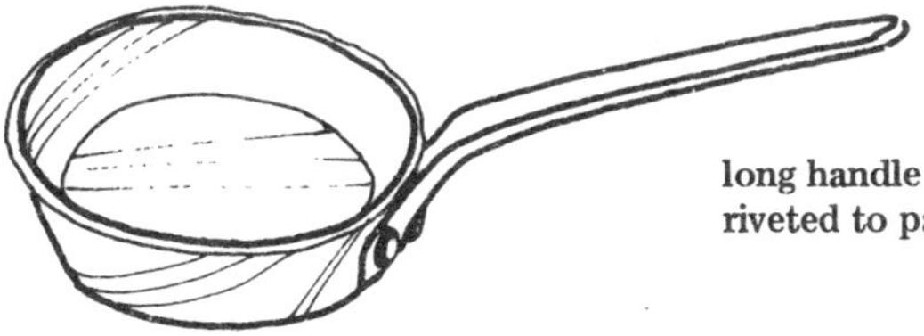

Figure 1.9 A good frying pan

A long-handled heavy-based, cast iron pan (figure 1.9) is ideal. A flimsy pan, on the other hand, causes foods to burn and cooks unevenly.

2

Cooking Eggs

Apart from the exciting culinary possibilities they offer, eggs are an excellent source of nourishment since they contain vitamins A and B, iron, fat and protein. However, the protein content is sensitive to heat and to being manipulated in various ways, and it is this property that largely determines culinary success or failure with egg dishes. A baked custard may be smooth or it may curdle and become lumpy; a cake may rise and sometimes fall afterwards; a meringue may come out of the oven crunchy or weepy: these are all examples of how the protein in eggs is capable of reacting.

In the United Kingdom, eggs popularly feature at breakfast or are used in simple, quick-to-prepare little dishes as a snack — a meal in themselves. In France, they are used more creatively, often forming part of an elaborate *hors d'oeuvre* in a formal meal, for example *oeufs mollets en gelée au jambon de Parme* (cold soft-boiled eggs in aspic with Parma ham) or *oeufs pochés à la tartare* (poached eggs with a macedoine of vegetables and mayonnaise).

The purpose of this chapter is twofold: first, to describe the part that eggs play in cookery and to discuss the problems that can occur; secondly, to describe how to cook eggs in simple ways by frying, poaching, boiling and so on.

Approximately 75 per cent of the egg is water, which evaporates through the porous shell as the egg deteriorates. A fresh egg thus feels heavier than a stale one. In place of the water, air enters, forming an air space in the fat end of the egg. This becomes larger in an older egg. It is seen when shelling a hard-boiled egg. Also noticeable in hard-boiled eggs prepared from stale eggs is ferrous sulphide. Ferrous sulphide is formed from the iron in the yolk combining with the sulphur in the white and shows up as a dark green ring between the yolk and the white. It is also responsible for the bad egg smell sometimes associated with hard-boiled eggs. The way to avoid this is to use fresh eggs and not to overcook them and to plunge them into cold running water as soon as they are done to prevent further cooking by residual heat. Another problem when preparing hard-boiled eggs is that the eggs sometimes crack on being lowered into the boiling water. We already know that eggs contain air and that air expands on heating, thus eggs used straight from the refrigerator are more likely to crack than those at room temperature, since a greater degree of expansion occurs. It is best to use eggs at room temperature or to warm them first by standing them in warm water. Older eggs are more likely to crack than new ones.

Poached eggs sometimes present problems. When cooked correctly, that is, in a pan of simmering water, the whites sometimes run away from the yolks rather than clinging gently together and around each yolk. A fresh egg contains a large amount of viscous white plus a smaller amount of thin white. With age, this thick viscous white becomes more and more watery. For this reason old eggs are not suitable for poaching — it is essential to use fresh ones that hold together in a good shape while they are gently simmered. (For the same reason, new eggs should be used for frying.) The addition of a little lemon juice or vinegar to the poaching liquid helps to keep the whites together.

On heating, the protein in egg coagulates, that is, it changes state, first becoming firm, then starting to become hard when heat is applied or if heated for too long. Because eggs harden with prolonged cooking or if fiercely cooked, all egg cookery should be gentle whatever method is used. Even hard-boiled eggs should not actually boil — they should really be simmered carefully for the minimum length of time necessary. 70 °C (156 °F) is the temperature at which egg coagulates, but when it is mixed with liquids or other ingredients, this coagulation temperature is raised. Thus, when mixed with milk as in a baked custard the coagulation temperature becomes 80 °C (176 °F) and when mixed with a greater amount of milk as in a stirred custard it becomes 85 °C (185 °F). The highest temperature for coagulation is about 88 °C (190 °F) whatever ingredients are used and in whatever quantity. When using a thermometer for a stirred custard, the custard should be removed from the heat several degrees below coagulation temperature because the egg will continue to cook in the residual heat. Stirring should continue for a few minutes after it is removed from the heat.

Fried eggs that are brown underneath with a crisp frilly edge are really overcooked: the fat was too hot. However, some people prefer their fried eggs this way, but overcooked scrambled eggs certainly have no appeal whatsoever. The effect here is that the water is squeezed out of the protein. Instead of being creamy in texture with large soft flakes it is watery and lumpy. When scrambling eggs, it is important to stir all the time, and also to stir at the right speed! The egg must have a certain time to coagulate on the bottom of the pan before it is stirred away for more uncooked egg to take its place. Cooked too fast, the texture is all wrong — the lumps of coagulated egg are too small. As in a stirred egg custard, scrambled egg should be removed from the heat before the last little bit of runny egg has set and while the egg is still shiny. Stirring should be continued for a second or two before turning on to a heated plate to serve.

Egg whites have the ability to entrap air bubbles and to form a foam. The yolks can also be whipped to a foam but to a lesser degree. You may have experienced an occasion when the whites have refused to whip up in the usual way, no matter how long you try. The most common reason for this is that a trace of the yolk has been incorporated into the whites or it may be that there was some grease in the bowl or on the whisk. There is nothing to remedy this. If you should get some yolk accidentally into the white the best thing to do is to neatly remove it with the half eggshell (this being the sharpest and thinnest and most suitable container you have at hand) before proceeding with whipping them up. When egg whites whip up to a foam they contain a large volume of air, with a lot of stretching required of the cell walls. As in most things, you can overdo it. Excessive whipping causes the cell walls to become over-distended and very fragile. If these same whites are subsequently to be folded into a sponge cake mixture, when the cake mixture goes into the oven, there is obviously going to be a great expansion of air and the whites cannot support it. The result is that the cake collapses. This is sometimes why what promises to be a really voluminous sponge cake collapses so disappointingly when removed from the oven. It is in the making of all kinds of meringue or other foam that the older eggs should be used as they contain more of the thin extensible white and they should be used warm. Normally, when egg whites are beaten to a foam they should be used immediately. If allowed to stand a while, they become liquid again and have to be re-beaten. However, to help stabilise them, a little acid added to the whites helps. This may be in the form of lemon juice or cream of tartar, which also help to bleach the white.

It has already been said that the degree to which the whites are whipped is important, and that if they are whipped too much the cell walls become so fragile that they eventually collapse. The first stage of beating will produce a liquid foam which becomes semi-liquid at the second stage and has coarse bubbles. It is at this semi-liquid stage that cream of tartar should be added, and also sugar, when making meringues. At stage three the whites form soft peaks when the beater is slowly lifted from the egg. The white does not flow any more. Towards the end of stage three the whites start to stand up stiffly. At the last stage, the whites become very dry and the foam can be cut into definite wedges. Egg whites used for cookery should never be allowed to reach this fourth and last stage. At this stage the cell walls have been stretched to their absolute limit and in consequence have been made fragile. Recognising these stages is very important in the making of meringue because failure to do so is often the cause of meringues going wrong. If the mixture becomes very gritty after adding the sugar, it is either because coarse granulated sugar was used which takes longer to dissolve, or, more likely, the whites were whipped for too long before the sugar was added, so that they became too dry to dissolve the sugar. When this happens, a teaspoon of water added to each egg white might do the trick. Caster sugar is usually recommended for meringues. It is, however, quite acceptable to use icing sugar. Icing sugar contains 15 per cent cornflour, and this helps to achieve a drier meringue. Should the meringues later develop beads of caramel while cooking, this is a sign that too much sugar has been added. If the meringues start to weep underneath then they have either been cooked too fast or the whites have been overbeaten.

It is quite interesting to note the different effects of cooking by gas compared with cooking by electricity because in cooking meringues we are essentially drying the meringues out. The atmosphere in a gas oven is more moist than that in an electric oven. I find that the old-fashioned drying cabinet often found in the cookery rooms of schools and adult education institutes gives the best results. *Dry* warm air is necessary *with* a draught. The atmosphere in a gas oven is often too moist for baking meringues and it is a good idea to leave the door of the oven slightly ajar. It is also preferable to bake them on thick brown paper lightly oiled, or on wood. A metal baking sheet becomes too hot and will overcook the meringues from underneath. Use old eggs for meringue making. You can store whites successfully in a covered jar in the refrigerator for this purpose for months. However, use at room temperature and, if possible, leave them uncovered in a cool place for 36 hours before proceeding. You can use any kind of beater — a hand whisk, rotary whisk or electric beater. A copper bowl is perfect in which to whip the foam (a small amount of acid comes from the metal) but most people make do without this lovely extravagance.

SCRAMBLED EGGS

Lightly beat together three eggs. Season with salt and pepper. You may add one tablespoon of cream or milk, which will make the scrambled eggs softer. In a medium sized saucepan heat 15 g of butter and when it begins to foam pour in the eggs. Use a wooden spoon to stir over a moderate heat. Make sure you stir right into the edges of the saucepan, and stir slowly to give the egg time to coagulate before it is moved away for more egg to replace it. Just before the last little bit of runny egg is coagulated, remove the pan from the heat but continue to stir for a second or two. The uncooked egg will coagulate in the heat of the pan. The finished scrambled eggs should be shiny and smooth. If they are watery you have overcooked them.

POACHED EGGS

Really fresh eggs are necessary for a perfect result by the traditional free-floating method. The whites then cling around and mask the yolk, giving a good oval shape. Pour water into a saucepan to a depth of at least 6 cm, adding one teaspoon of salt and one dessertspoon of vinegar for each 500 ml of water used. (This gives flavour and helps the whites to bunch.) Bring to the boil. Break the eggs one at a time into a cup then slide individually into the boiling water — now turned down to the barest simmer. Poach for 3 minutes. Remove with a slotted spoon. Serve on hot buttered toast. If the eggs are required for a cold dish they should be plunged into cold water as soon as they come from the pan to stop further cooking.

BOILED EGGS

Use eggs at room temperature, otherwise they will crack when lowered into the water if straight from the refrigerator. Two further ways of ensuring that an egg does not crack as it is lowered into the simmering water is, first, to pierce the fat end where the air space is with a pin. This allows the expanding air to escape easily. Secondly, the egg can be placed in a basin of warm water for a few minutes before cooking so that the degree of subsequent expansion is not so great. The water should be simmering, not boiling. A medium egg lowered into simmering water will soft-boil in about 4 minutes. To hard-boil allow 10 minutes. Hard-boiled eggs should be cooled immediately under cold water when done to prevent the formation of ferrous sulphide, seen as a green ring between the yolk and the white.

BAKED EGGS

Break the eggs carefully into individual well-buttered cocotte dishes, season with salt and pepper and bake in the middle of a regulo 4, 180 °C (350 °F) oven until the whites are coagulated and the yolks still soft. The time will be about 10 minutes. You can vary it by adding a spoonful of thick cream, or lining each cocotte with thin slivers of cheese, or by putting a spoonful of fried onion or bacon into each one before the eggs are added. It is important not to overcook them—the yolks must remain soft.

FRIED EGGS

It is essential to use very fresh eggs for frying so that the thick viscous white clings around the yolk. Bacon fat is a popular medium to use, otherwise use butter. There should be sufficient fat to cover the bottom of a heavy-based frying pan to 2 to 3 mm and it should be hot when the eggs are carefully broken into it. The heat should then be lowered to coagulate the whites without making them hard. The fat can be spooned over the yolks, which will change their colour as the film of white coagulates around them, or they can be left a bright yellow. Some people prefer to add a teaspoon of water to each egg, then cover the frying pan with a lid so that the top of the egg coagulates under steam. Or, instead of basting or covering the pan with a lid, the eggs can be carefully flipped upside down very briefly just before serving.

OMELETTE

Beat together three eggs until mixed but not foamy in a basin. Season with salt and pepper and, to make the mixture lighter, you can add up to 3 tablespoons of liquid—water, milk or cream. In a heavy-based omelette pan heat a knob of butter, swirling it around to cover the bottom of the pan in a thin film. There should not be excessive fat. Pour the eggs into the foaming butter, then, after a few seconds, use a wooden spoon to lift the coagulated egg on one side, allowing the still-runny egg to flow beneath. Do this several times around the edge of the pan until there is no more liquid egg. The whole process should take 30 seconds or just over. Use a spatula to loosen around the edges. Hold the pan above a warmed serving plate in a vertical position so that the omelette rolls over and out of the pan. Serve immediately. Any fillings which are to be incorporated beforehand should be warmed in a separate pan alongside.

SOUFFLÉ

The dish in which a soufflé is cooked should have straight sides and be buttered so liberally that the expanding foam slides easily up the greasy sides as it bakes and stands proudly above. A soufflé is made from a thick panada sauce into which egg yolks and the flavouring are beaten. The whites whipped to a foam are folded in and the mixture is then baked. (A panada is simply a white sauce of a binding consistency about twice as thick as the normal sauce used for coating foods.) For a sweet soufflé, a cornflour thickened sauce is more frequently used. It is most important that the whites are not beaten so much that they become over-distended, otherwise the additional expansion in the oven will cause them to finally collapse. Soufflés should be served immediately they come from the oven.

Separating the yolk from the white of an egg is usually done because the white has to be whipped to a foam. If this is the case, make sure that you have a perfectly clean bowl in which to drop the whites, bearing in mind that if there is any trace of grease the whites will not whip up. Hold the egg firmly in the right hand and tap it firmly two or three times on the edge of a bowl so that the eggshell is cracked half way round its middle. In the left hand hold the egg upright and lift the top half of shell completely away. The egg yolk will remain in the bottom half of the shell while the white dribbles out through your fingers (figure 2.1). This does not feel very nice but it is the way to do it. Now tip the yolk into the empty half of the shell—quickly—and the remaining white will dribble away. (If you tip the yolk slowly from one half-shell to the other, it will break because the sharp edge of the shell will cut into it.)

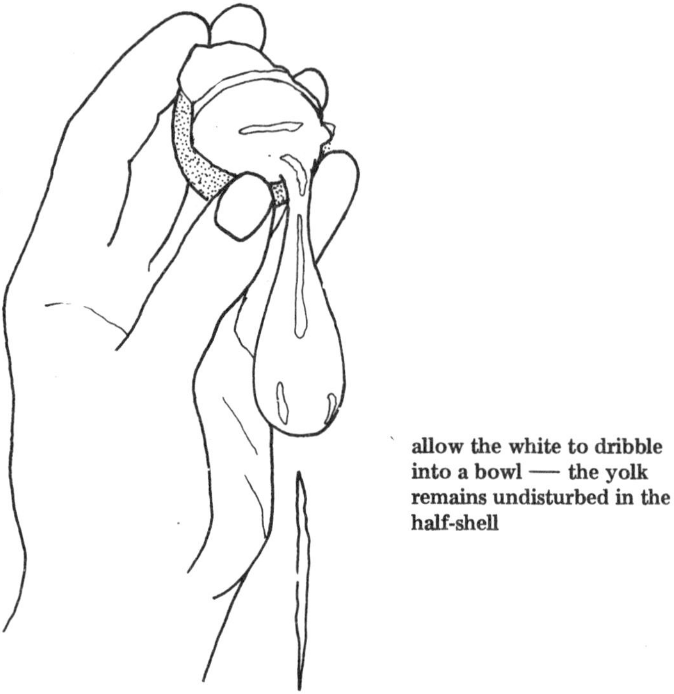
allow the white to dribble
into a bowl — the yolk
remains undisturbed in the
half-shell

Figure 2.1 How to separate the yolk from the white of an egg

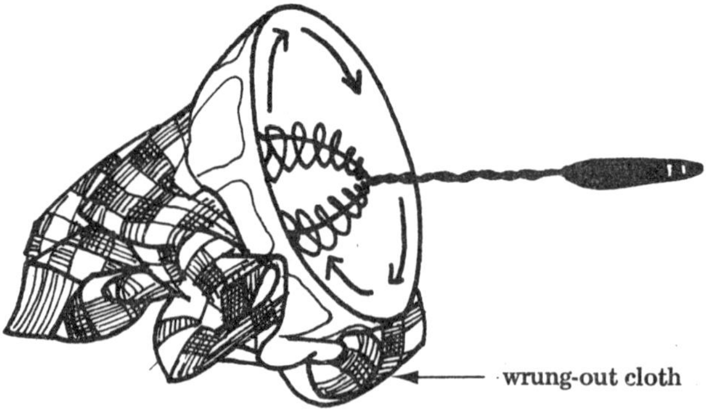
wrung-out cloth

Figure 2.2 Whisking eggs or cream

When whisking with a hand-whisk (or beating a mixture with a wooden spoon), stand the bowl on a wrung-out cloth, which will steady it: this makes an enormous amount of difference to the ease with which the job can be done (figure 2.2). Tip the bowl on its side and hold with the left hand while you whisk or beat with the other. Whisking should be done in a circular motion that actually lifts the egg whites or cream into the air so that air is incorporated into it.

Cheese Soufflé

50 g butter; 50 g flour; 275 ml milk; 5 egg yolks; 125 g Cheddar cheese; ½ teaspoon made mustard; salt and pepper; 6 egg whites.

Preheat the oven to regulo 6, 200 °C (400 °F). Stand a metal baking sheet on the middle shelf of the oven to get hot; this will help to start cooking the soufflé when it is ready to go in. Brush the inside of a 1 litre soufflé dish liberally with soft butter. Separate the eggs. Make a thick white sauce by first heating the butter in a pan and stirring in the flour to make a roux. Cook this roux for several minutes without allowing it to brown, using a wooden spoon to stir constantly as you do so. Remove from the heat and add the milk a little at a time, stirring well between each addition and the next until it is all used up. Return to the heat and slowly bring to the boil, stirring, when it will have become very thick. Grate the cheese. Add the yolks and the cheese to the now slightly cooled sauce and beat well. Add the mustard and season with salt and pepper. In a large bowl whisk the whites until they just hold peaks, but no more than this. Take a tablespoonful of the whites and beat into the thick sauce (this will loosen the sauce ready for the whites). Using a spatula, carefully fold the remaining whites into the mixture. Turn the mixture into the prepared dish, smooth the top and bake for 30 to 35 minutes, when the soufflé should be well risen and golden brown. [*Serves 4*]

MAYONNAISE

Egg yolks have the ability to form an emulsion with oil. The mustard helps form this emulsion.

> *1 egg yolk; a pinch each of salt, pepper and dry mustard; up to 275 ml oil; 1 lemon; additional seasoning to your taste.*

Put the egg yolk into a clean basin and add to it the salt, pepper and mustard. Stir well for about 15 seconds. Add a few drops of oil and stir with a wooden spoon. In doing this, you may be surprised to find that the mixture does not become thinner with the addition of the oil, but suddenly you may have a very thick mixture. When it becomes thick, thin it with a few drops of lemon juice. Then continue adding the oil a few drops at a time and alternate with the lemon juice as it becomes thick again. As time goes on you may start to add the oil in dribbles rather than in drops as you did to start with. Continue in this way until all the oil is used up. (One egg yolk can 'absorb' up to *275 ml* of oil but you can use less than this if you wish.) Taste the mayonnaise. Many people who make mayonnaise for the first time complain that it tastes 'oily'. You can remedy this by adding a teaspoon of icing sugar, which seems to do the trick, and which most people prefer. You may also need to season with additional salt, pepper and mustard. For a sharper mayonnaise use vinegar instead of, or in addition to, lemon juice. If the mixture separates out into lumps you can remedy it by starting with another egg yolk in another basin and adding the curdled mixture to it as if it were the oil. Continue until all the curdled mixture has been taken up by the second yolk, which it will do smoothly. Making mayonnaise should take about 10 minutes.

A BAKED CUSTARD

This is a sweetened milk and egg mixture which is baked until it is set. Cream may replace some of the milk. Nutmeg is sometimes grated over the top of it before baking. The texture should be absolutely smooth, without holes, and soft yet firm. Two large eggs will set 1 litre of liquid, but usually there are more eggs in proportion to milk than this. Egg yolks alone make a firmer and more creamy custard than do whole eggs. Egg whites can be used alone but will give a less firm custard than whole eggs. Egg custards are usually baked standing in a *bain-marie*, which maintains a steady temperature. Otherwise, if it becomes too hot, the mixture curdles, that is, the water is squeezed out of the protein and it becomes a lumpy watery mess. Custards should not be baked faster than at regulo 4, 180 °C (350 °F). A custard is done when its centre is seen to wobble slightly when the dish is given a slight jerk. There should be no indication of any flow remaining beneath the skin that has formed. A custard removed from the oven will continue to cook a little in the residual heat, so may be removed just before it is completely set.

Figure 2.3 A *bain-marie*

Any suitable ovenproof container (figure 2.3) can be used —a dish or a roasting tin—as a *bain-marie* (water bath) in which certain foods, for example custards and some pâtés, are baked.

ZABAGLIONE

Italian. It replaces the egg nog as a revitaliser. In the United Kingdom it is often included as a pudding on the menus of Italian restaurants, and is best cooked at table and eaten hot, accompanied by *langues de chat* biscuits.

Zabaglione should really be made in the special copper pan of the same name held directly over the heat. However, a basin standing over a pan of boiling water will do if you do not mind the finished product being less hot on serving than it should be. I watched an Italian cook making this and he used half eggshells to measure the ingredients — a neat method, described below.

3 egg yolks; 1 half eggshell caster sugar; 4 half eggshells Marsala.

Put two large wine goblets to warm through. Stand a basin containing all the ingredients over a pan of boiling water and whisk constantly until it forms a foam and then comes 'to the ribbon' (that is, it leaves a trail from the whisk and just begins to hold its own shape). Immediately divide between the two glasses and serve accompanied by sponge fingers or, better still, *langues de chat* biscuits.

Note that the yolks alone are responsible for producing the foam, not the whites, which are usually associated with this type of light mixture in other dishes. When using the proper copper pan, it should be held directly over the flame, producing a closer-textured, firmer and hotter zabaglione.

[*Serves 2*]

3

Soups

The word 'stock' could well have replaced this chapter heading. Stock is the basis of all good soups (gravies, sauces and casseroles) and, although cookery books in general provide a wide variety of individual soup recipes, it is as well to understand the basics because this will give you freedom to develop your own ideas. Stock is the extraction of gelatine and soluble and stimulating flavours from bones, meat, vegetables, fish and aromatics dissolved in water. The bones, etc., are simmered in water for many hours (with the exception of fish which would become bitter) to extract the maximum amount of flavourings. The liquid is then strained through a sieve or through muslin and retained for use, while the solids are discarded, although the meat and vegetables are sometimes retained for certain soups, and may be added later as a garnish — as in a broth — or they may be sieved to make a purée-type soup such as *vichyssoise*. There are several types of stock: white stock (veal based), chicken stock, brown stock (beef based), game stock, vegetable and fish. One of these is necessary to every soup, depending on its type. Thus, *vichyssoise* has a basis of light chicken stock, *soupe à l'oignon* is made with brown stock, and so on. Delicate flavoured vegetable soups are made from a white or a chicken stock, and not from a vegetable stock as you might expect — vegetable stock is useful in the making of vegetarian soups.

In some households soups are produced as a matter of course, forming part of a routine. For others, soups only come out of tins, and this habit is widespread for many reasons. Today's grandmothers include the many women who abandoned the kitchen and went out to work when their children were young—so what they themselves had absorbed from their mothers regarding kitchen and food management was not passed on to their daughters. The same thing happened to the daughters in their turn, but in this case there was no knowledge to pass on anyway, since the only person previously to practise the old customs and skills was great-grandmother. So part of what is missing in today's kitchens is the stockpots from which all great soups come, whatever their style — from fine consommés to country-style broths. Stockpots have to be managed, and this involves time and space (which many people do not have), as well as knowing what to put in them. They are not to be regarded as some kind of disposal pot for leftovers.

Soups are made throughout the world and it is soup-making by the peasant folk of any country that is seen as the best method of making what little they do have go a long way. Such hearty concoctions form the meal itself and are not simply the overture to it. But in the modern world not all soups are economical and filling, nor are they intended as such. Consommés are intended for the start of a meal — stimulating the appetite only, not satisfying it. Thick and nourishing ones are best served informally for lunch or supper — perhaps accompanied by bread and cheese.

We have seen that there are different kinds of stock. Soups are also variously classified, and simply put they are: consommés, cleared soups made of beef, chicken or game stock; broths, uncleared meat and vegetable stocks which usually contain the pieces of meat and vegetables from which they are made with the addition of rice, barley or pasta; and thirdly — thickened soups, which are sometimes termed cream soups, yet do not necessarily contain cream. These thick soups have a creamy consistency. They may be thickened in various ways, by puréeing the stock ingredients of the liquid, by adding a flour liaison, or by adding an egg yolk and cream liaison just before serving. The last method makes a very rich soup. Often, two of these methods are used together, for example, a puréed celery soup needs an additional starch liaison to keep the purée in suspension. A puréed lentil soup on the other hand requires no further starch liaison.

In the United Kingdom, a home-made chicken broth is

frequently made following a roast chicken meal, since the ingredients for the stock present themselves ready at hand. These are the carcase, the giblets, onion, carrot, celery, a bay-leaf, a few peppercorns, salt and water. If these are all put into a pan and simply simmered together and strained the result is a rather crude stock-cum-soup that many people accept as chicken broth. This can be improved by using a few extra items, and preparing them in a slightly different way.

CHICKEN STOCK—CHICKEN BROTH

Stock: 2 kg bones (carcase, giblets, one or two bacon rinds or a ham bone, plus a veal knuckle); 4 l water; bouquet garni; 10 peppercorns; 3 cloves; ½ kg mixed vegetables (onion, leek, carrot, celery, plus a very little parsnip and turnip); Garnish: 1 tablespoon rice; chopped parsley.

Place the bones in the stockpot with the water and bring slowly to the boil. Turn down to simmer. As the scum rises to the surface, remove it with a perforated spoon until no more is seen. Add the *bouquet garni* and spices and continue simmering for 5 to 6 hours. Meanwhile clean the vegetables but leave whole. Add to the stockpot with the bones for the final hour. Strain the stock into a clean bowl through a sieve or through muslin and leave in a cool place to set overnight. Reserve the vegetables (which should be tender without being overdone). Discard the *bouquet garni* and spices. Pull any pieces of chicken from the bones and reserve these with the vegetables. Discard bones, rinds and giblets. Next day, use a spoon to scrape the fat from the top of the jellied stock. Return the stock to the stockpot, bring to the boil and reduce if more concentration of flavour is required. Toss in the rice and cook for about 20 minutes. Just before serving, return the pieces of chicken and vegetables to the broth and heat completely through. Garnish with chopped parsley.

Note that in the above recipe, a knuckle of veal is included, which imparts a lot of gelatine to the stock when simmered slowly and for a long time. The bacon rinds give flavour, but they must be used with discretion or the flavour will predominate. In fact, no single ingredient should stand out apart from the intended chicken flavour itself. Be careful with strongly flavoured vegetables such as the turnip or the parsnip used here — again, use only a small amount. The vegetables in the above recipe are added to the stock for a short time towards the end of cooking so they will be tender, not overdone, and can therefore be used as a garnish to the soup later on. For a stock in which the vegetables are eventually discarded, they are added not before 2 hours after the stock has started. The vegetables should not be allowed to cook for as long as the meat and bones. If the vegetables are allowed to cook for too long, they start to absorb the flavours in the stock rather than impart flavour to it. All the scum should be removed from any stock before the vegetables are added; in any case, the vegetables float on the surface so they would only make the job of skimming more difficult if added at the beginning. In the above recipe, the fat (and there is always some fat no matter how careful one is in trimming it) is allowed to cool along with the stock, so that next day it can easily be scraped away. This is the easiest and surest way of degreasing, and is most important for the success of the soup. Have you ever burnt your mouth on a greasy soup? If you are in a hurry, however, and are unable to wait for the stock to cool, the fat can be removed using absorbent kitchen paper.

WHITE STOCK

The ingredients for white stock are almost identical to those for chicken stock, as in the previous recipe, except that there is a different emphasis on the choice of bones.

2 kg bones (knuckle of veal plus a selection from neck of mutton, chicken carcase, chicken feet, calf's foot, ham bone); 4 l water; bouquet garni; 10 peppercorns; 3 cloves; ½ kg mixed vegetables (onion, leek, carrot, celery, plus a very little parsnip or turnip).

The method for making it remains the same. Briefly it is as follows. Put bones in stockpot and slowly bring to the boil. Turn down to simmer. Cook bones for 5 to 6 hours. Remove all scum from the surface of the water. Add the *bouquet garni* and the spices. After 2 or 3 hours add the vegetables, whole. After the bones have cooked, strain and allow to go cold. Skim fat from the surface. Use as required.

BROWN STOCK

The proportions of meat bones to vegetables for a brown stock are the same as for chicken and white stock. You would, however, use a shin of beef for it plus a veal knuckle and a ham bone. You could use all beef instead of bones but this is expensive to do. The selection of vegetables is the same for chicken, white and beef stocks. For the darker beef stock you can also include tomatoes and mushrooms, which you could not use in the other two. The general method for making a brown stock is slightly different from that for white and chicken stocks in that the meat, bones and vegetables are browned before being placed in the stockpot. This is done by placing the bones in one layer in a roasting pan and putting at the top of a very hot oven; the bones should be turned over as they brown to do the other side. The bones are drained of any fat and placed in the stockpot ready to proceed. The roasting pan will now contain meat juices and fat (drippings). The fat should be poured off and the pan deglazed with a cup of water; scrape in the brown bits with a wooden spoon as you do so. This water is added to the stockpot. Vegetables and meat are browned in a little fat in a frying pan, taking approximately 5 minutes to brown.

2 kg beef or beef and bones (use shin or neck of beef, a knuckle of veal and a ham bone); 4 l water; ½ kg vegetables (onion, carrot, leek, celery, plus a very little parsnip and turnip); fat for browning; bouquet garni; 10 peppercorns; 3 cloves.

Brown the bones in a roasting pan in a hot oven. Place in stockpot with water. Cut up the meat and brown in a little fat in a frying pan. Transfer to stockpot and allow to soak with bones for ½ hour. Meanwhile, deglaze both pans and add the juices to the stockpot. Cut up the vegetables roughly and brown in a little fat in the frying pan. Set aside. Bring the water slowly to the boil. Turn down to simmer, and cook the bones for 5 to 6 hours. Remove the scum as it rises from the meat. Add the *bouquet garni* and the spices. After 2 or 3 hours add the vegetables whole. When the bones are cooked strain and allow to go cold. Next day, use a spoon to scrape the fat from the top of the jellied stock. Use the stock as required.

For game stock proceed as for brown stock, using a mixture of game bones and shin of beef. A few small pieces of game can be included.

For vegetable stock dried pulse vegetables (peas and beans) soaked overnight can be used in addition to the usual fresh root vegetables used in other stocks. They need cooking only for 3 to 4 hours.

The recipe for fish stock can be found on p. 50 in chapter 5.

There remain a few dos and don'ts regarding stockmaking and possible questions left unanswered.

How can the maximum flavour be obtained from stock ingredients? To get the best out of bones, meat and vegetables, the bones and meat need to be cut up small so there is more surface area out of which the flavours can be extracted. When making a brown stock, the browned ingredients should be allowed to soak in the water before proceeding to bring to the boil. Simmer the bones for 5 to 6 hours at least. It is during this time that most of the flavours are extracted. You can simmer the bones for longer than this but not so much flavour will be extracted.

Is there anything one might be tempted to add to the stockpot that shouldn't be added? In the ordinary kitchen there are presumably several items — leftovers included — which find their way into the stockpot and should not be there. The water in which green vegetables have been cooked will make a stock bitter. Potatoes, rice, bread and barley should be excluded — these will cloud the liquid, as will any left-over gravies or sauces thickened with flour or cornflour; also, these will encourage the stock to turn sour, especially in summer. Do not be encouraged to add anything that has the slightest suspicion of deterioration about it — all ingredients must be really wholesome. Avoid pieces of fat meat.

You can add leftover bits of lean meat, gristle and skin, and any plain liquids that meat has been cooked in.

How is it possible to get a really clear stock? It is careful skimming in the early stages that counts, and if there is a large amount of scum, the whole lot can be poured off right at the beginning, and fresh water added, that is, blanching. After that, keep the liquid at a very bare simmer—if it boils fast, any scum will break up and mix in. You may also add some broken egg shell, which helps to keep it clear. It also helps if you keep the vegetables whole and remove them from the simmering stock before they disintegrate.

Does it matter how much vegetable to meat there is? Too many vegetables simmered for too long will make the stock sour, while too many of any one kind will predominate. Also, when making stock to keep rather than for immediate use, make it without the vegetables as these encourage it to ferment. A smaller amount of vegetables can then be cut up and simmered with the stock as needed.

For how long will stock keep? It is said that, in China, there are stocks going today which were started hundreds of years ago! that is, they are used and replenished daily, but are never allowed to run dry. (This is not to be understood as a recommendation.) All stocks should be boiled up daily in summer, and once every two days in winter provided they are kept in a cool place. Any additions to an old stock should all be added together and simmered for a proper length of time, that is, scraps should not be added just at any time. A stock that has cooled and set with its layer of fat on top, if not for immediate use, should be stored as it is; the layer of fat helps exclude the air, and thus helps preserve it. In any event, it should be stored in a clean bowl, and not allowed to stand in the pot in which it was made, and certainly not near the warm cooker. If too much stock has been made to store easily, it can be condensed into what is called a meat glaze; in this form it will keep for weeks in the refrigerator. Start by boiling the stock in a large pan until it becomes well reduced and much thicker, then transfer to a smaller pan, and continue at a lower heat until it becomes syrup-like. Pour into a clean jar and allow to set. Store covered with a lid or with a film of butter poured over the top.

4

Pâtés

The making of pâtés represented one of the original methods of preserving meat before refrigeration techniques, but pâté is now made and eaten simply because people like it. In France it is part of the gastronomic culture. It is open to infinite variation, is easy to make (although not all pâtés are necessarily quick to prepare), and provides a popular lunch or supper dish to be eaten with toast or bread, or is used as a starter to a meal, or incorporated into a cold mixed *hors d'oeuvre*. Most pâtés keep well — for up to 10 days under refrigeration, and can be made to keep longer if wished.

However, many people remain puzzled over the difference between a pâté and a terrine. Confusion arises after being served a *terrine maison* in a restaurant, which to all intents and purposes is identical to a *pâté de campagne* made at home from a cookery book recipe. In defining this difference — and having said earlier that pâtés were made long before modern times — it should be mentioned that these two words are strangely absent from the indexes of old English cookery books. However, close to them in meaning are the words tureen and patty. Although a tureen is now understood to be a container for soup, it used to describe potted meats and the dish that held them. The not dissimilar French word *terrine*, coming from the Latin *terra*, earth, also describes a glazed earthen pot in which ground meat is cooked. The English word patty or pattie describes a little pastry pie, and this is similar to the French *pâté*, which correctly means meat or fish, ground, and enclosed on all sides by pastry — a pie! It is also near to the word *pâte* meaning paste. Through misusage of these words both here and in France their meaning has become less clear. Pâté is now used to describe not only the moulded pie it once meant, but also the same meat mixture when baked in a dish lined with bacon or pork fat. The latter should really be called a terrine. To clarify, one could refer to *pâté en croûte*, or *pâté en terrine*.

The popularity of glazed earthenware terrines in the last century became such that Wedgwood and Spode were among those producing pots resembling pork pies — which became popularly known as pie-crust pottery. In France, similar pots are still made; they are very expensive, and can be viewed in Harrods and the General Trading Company, Sloane Street. They have lids fashioned into pheasants and hare, while the roughened and golden brown container resembles the pastry walls.

A *pâté en croûte* closely resembles the English raised pies of which pork, and veal-and-ham are the most popular. The English versions commonly available are simpler in that all the meats are ground together, and so less interesting when cut, but this should not be allowed to belie the excellent flavour of many of them. In the French pies, there is more play with colours, with textures and with the flavours of two or more meats which may be cubed, chopped, minced and finely sliced, all in the one pie. There may be further additions, of green pistachio nuts, of little firm mushrooms and of truffle parings. A second difference is the pastry: the French use *pâte brisée* (a kind of shortcrust) while the English pies with their malleable hot water crust pastry could be either made in a tinned mould, or formed by hand. When cooled, these hand-raised pastry cases set hard, then the filling is put in, the lid fixed and decorated, and all that is needed is a supporting band of greaseproof paper while they bake. Actually this type of pastry was not originally meant to be eaten; it was simply a lean flour and water crust containing little fat meant as a disposable casing for the meats. However, by making the pastry richer by increasing the proportion of fat it becomes really delicious — crunchy on the outside while the inside absorbs all the seasoned juices from the meats. Many commercial pies have the most excellent crunchy crusts that set a good example to the home cook.

So far, we have seen that the word pâté is, by common usage, a meat mixture cooked either in a pie crust or in a terrine. In addition it can also be stuffed inside a boned-out chicken or duck and become a *galantine de volaille* or *galantine de canard*. And if this galantine is wrapped in pastry and baked, the result would become a *pâté de canard en croûte.*

Although the Greeks and Egyptians made pâté, it is the French who are now world famous for it, with each region having its own indigenous variation reflecting the meats readily available, the local liquor and the herbs of that area. It is from Périgord that the finest and most expensive pâté of all comes — *pâté de foie gras* — made from the livers of specially fattened geese or ducks (the goose livers weighing anything up to 1½ kg), with cognac and the black truffles of the region. In Provence it is likely to incorporate snails and thrushes, wild hare and venison, in Touraine pork and ham. In Burgundy, marc is used and in Armagnac, south-east of Bordeaux, the spirit of the same name.

The pâtés reviewed so far are those made of raw ground meat which is then cooked in a crust or a terrine. In addition, there are pâtés made by mincing, pounding or blending cooked meats which are seasoned and mixed with melted butter, then poured into little cocottes or ramekins to set. These are called potted meats — a term which has become unfashionable — and of which only potted shrimps are likely to be seen in restaurants. There are also pâtés made of vegetables, and of smoked fish, and there is a popular cheese and tinned consommé blend which sets mousse-like on chilling.

A selection of potted meats and other types of pâté recipes is included at the end of the chapter.

Traditional meat pâtés start basically with lean pork, pork fat, liquor, seasonings and eggs. This basis is sometimes referred to as a *farce* (stuffing) and can be rough or smooth, depending how finely it is ground. A smooth pâté should have a finished texture of cream or curd cheese. One type of pâté is referred to as *fromage de tête*, which is another name for brawn, meaning sheep's head cheese. A farce (stuffing) often includes minced veal for adding lightness. Into this farce can go livers, pieces of game, bacon, slices of ham and tongue. Bacon or any salt pork tends to give the finished pâté a rosy glow from the saltpetre in the curing process, and will change the texture and flavour. The bacon can be smoked or green, but must not be used in excess, otherwise the flavour will be ruined. In game pâtés, there should not be more than about 25 per cent of this strong meat in the total weight.

A professional pâté includes a good proportion of fresh pork fat. The reason for the failure of many pâtés is that the cook has failed to observe this point, and the finished pâté will not have the right flavour, and will be dry and crumbly, without adhesion. Commercial pâtés and pork pies include a lot of fat. Just how the fat is distributed does not matter: it can be by lining the inside surface of the terrine (figure 4.1)

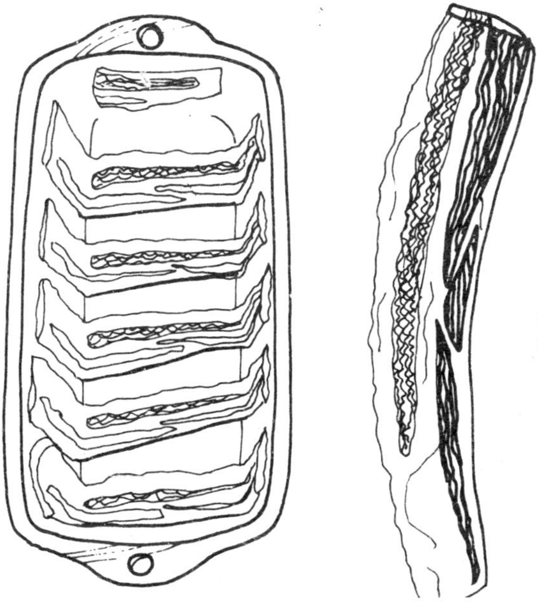

Figure 4.1 How to line a pâté dish with bacon

and covering the top of the mixture with strips of bacon or with thin sheets of pork fat *(bardes de lard)*, or by adding melted butter or lard to the raw mixture, or layering strips of *lard gras* within the meats. The best kind of fat to use is *lard gras.* It comes from just under the skin of the loin of the pig, and is white, firm, and capable of being cut into thin sheets *(bardes de lard)* or in long neat strips *(lardons)* for larding. There should be as much fat as lean including these lining strips. *Lard gras* will add smoothness and make the pâté soft and spreadable. In English butchers' shops it is not easy to obtain *lard gras*, which is why bacon is often called for in recipes instead. Another alternative is belly pork, or fat from the leg or inside the loin (flair fat). Bacon may need to be blamched (simmered) for 10 minutes initially to remove excess salt. In some instances, sausage meat is used in place of fat, either to line the dish, or to mix in. The recipe *pâté de chagny* uses sausage meat—there is no mincing—making it a very quick recipe to prepare.

Once a pâté is baked it is impossible to alter the seasonings, which should therefore be judged in the raw stage. This is easily done by frying a spoonful of the mixture in the corner of a frying pan (not in salted butter, however) using a little lard. Bear in mind that cold food has less flavour than warm food — so season well. It is in the blending of the ingredients and the seasoning of them that the imagination and skill of the cook is of utmost importance. Seasonings include a selection of bay, thyme, juniper berries, mace, garlic, lemon, pepper and salt, and one or more liquors, such as white wine, brandy, dry madeira, port and sherry— these are the most common. Sometimes the meats are marinated in the liquor to tenderise them. In any case, a pâté is best left to stand for a few hours or overnight before baking to allow the flavours to penetrate.

Eggs are incorporated to bind it together, while a spoonful of flour will make a pâté firmer, as also will a few fresh white breadcrumbs or a little meat jelly, and, when cooked, the pâté may be pressed to give it a closer texture and better shape and to make cutting easier. A little thick cream is sometimes incorporated to give a soft texture.

Pâtés can be cooked in any ovenproof vessel of suitable shape and size — a soufflé dish, loaf tin, foil container, Pyrex bowl, or a terrine specially made for the purpose which may be of glazed earthenware or enamelled cast iron such as those made by Le Creuset. If the container is attractive enough the pâté can be served from it, otherwise it should be turned out on to a plate, revealing the pink lining strips of bacon which some people prefer to see anyway.

The dish in which the pâté is cooked must be covered, either by its own lid or with foil or both. There is no need to use the luting paste (flour and water) to seal the lid as recommended in some recipes of older cookery books. It is then set in a *bain-marie* (a roasting tin will do) to ensure a gentle moist atmosphere, the water coming about 3 cm up the sides. Start with boiling water so that the contents start warming up immediately. If cold water is poured in, the recommended cooking time will need to be increased. The time will also depend on the shape and size of the dish. Oven temperatures do vary between recipes according to the nature of the ingredients. Coarsely cut meat will take longer. Livers cook more quickly than pork. To test whether a pâté is cooked first remove it from the oven and observe whether it has shrunk away from the sides, which should have occurred. Secondly, tilt the pâté to one side and see whether the juices that run out are clear, or still pink, indicating that it is still raw. When nearly done, it can be replaced in the oven without its cover at a higher temperature to brown the top. You may not want this, however, especially if it is eventually to be unmoulded. Do not overcook. A cooked pâté should still be pinkish inside and this misleads some into thinking that it is still raw. It is the colour of the juices that counts. Another indication that a fat pâté is cooked is that the juices are bubbling around the edges.

When the terrine is done, allow it to cool for about an hour, then put a weight on top to make it firmer for cutting and a better shape. If a container the same size and shape as the terrine (pâté dish) is available, this is ideal to use. First cover the surface of the pâté with a piece of aluminium foil or greaseproof paper, then fit the empty container over it and weight down with cans of food or weights (figure 4.2). A board or plate that fits the terrine on which to support the weights can be used instead.

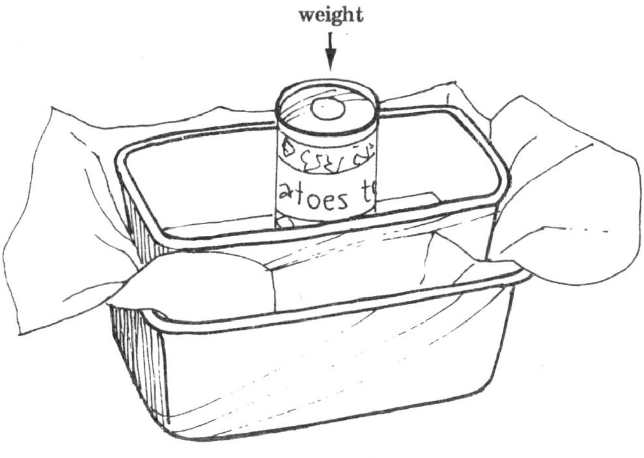

Figure 4.2 Weighting down a pâté

When completely cold it can be filled up with cooled liquid aspic if for immediate use, or with melted butter or lard if it is to be kept. In any case a pâté should be kept for at least 2 days to allow the flavours to develop. It is best from a culinary point of view to make the aspic (if used) from the bones and trimmings; a quick alternative is to use the commercial crystals as instructed on the packet, and a squeeze of lemon or a little sherry can be added. Decorations can be laid on to the aspic or lard surface. Often these indicate what the contents are, for instance, slices of orange would do well on a pâté made with duck flavoured with port and orange. Examples of decorating pâtés are given on p. 35.

A pâté to be unmoulded from its cooking vessel, perhaps because the vessel is not attractive enough to place on the table (or for any other reason), can be served in several ways. It can simply be turned out on to a plate and garnished with lettuce. Or a slightly larger container than the one in which it was cooked can be lined with aspic, cooled, the pâté placed on top of it and the sides filled up with more cooled but still liquid aspic. Unmould when cold. If a definite number of people are to be served from one pâté, another alternative is to slice it first and arrange on a plate with the slices overlapping to ensure that there is enough for everyone. If it is a main course serve with green salad, gherkins and fresh crusty bread or hot toast. A pâté is concentrated meat, so if if is to be a starter to a meal, go steady with the size of servings, otherwise there will be no room left to eat and enjoy the rest of the meal.

Some garnishes are suited to being applied before the pâté is baked (bayleaves, bacon, peppercorns), while others are better put on afterwards (parsley, orange segments) (figure 4.3). The surface of the pâté can then be glazed with liquid aspic poured on when it has cooled.

It is not recommended that pâtés are made to put in the freezer. A thawed-out pâté has a damp quality about it which never regains the original creamy texture. If it must be made for keeping, the following method is an alternative. Remove the cold pâté from the terrine, scraping off fat and meat juices, and remove the bacon rinds. Dry it by wiping with kitchen paper or a cloth. Wash out the terrine and dry that, then replace the meat. Pour into it cooled melted lard to cover the pâté by 1 cm and allow to set. Cover with a sheet of foil, pressing well down on to the surface of the fat.

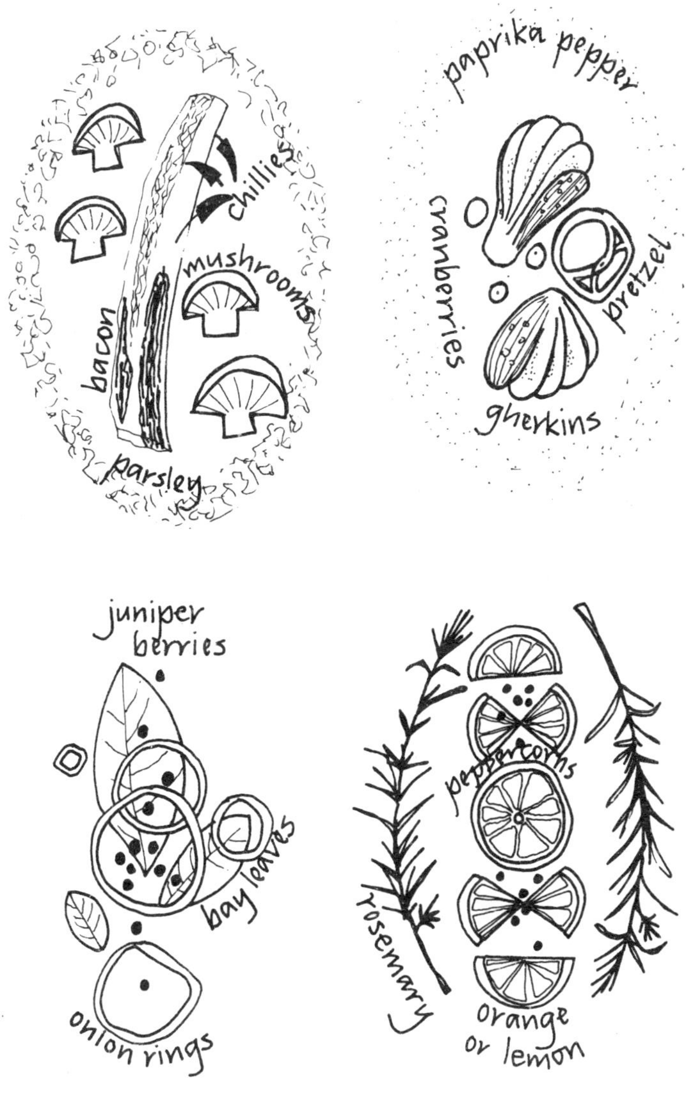

Figure 4.3 Ways of decorating a pâté

Cover with a second double layer over the entire dish itself. The point is not to allow any air to reach the pâté in any way and it is most important that the terrine is scrupulously clean. It should then be stored in a very cool and dry place, or in the refrigerator. This is an old method of keeping pâtés; they were kept by this method from one year to the next.

For seasoning pâtés and terrines, a spice mix called *quatre-épices* ('four spices') is used by the French for convenience since it is quicker to open one spice jar than four. It is similar to the English mixed spice, which is a handy way of flavouring cakes and puddings, and to the Indian combination called *garam masala*, used in curries and other spiced savoury dishes. *Quatre-épices* can be adjusted to your taste. The usual ingredients are as follows.

QUATRE-ÉPICES

French spice mix for pâtés, and all manner of *charcuterie.*

25 g ground cloves; 25 g ground nutmeg; 25 g ground cinnamon or ginger; 175 g ground black pepper.

Mix together and store in small airtight jars.

TERRINE MAISON

A traditional-style pâté incorporating minced and sliced meats, whole chicken livers and brandy, which is then spiced, seasoned and baked in a large terrine lined with thin sheets of pork fat. It is not difficult to make but the preparation is lengthy.

500 g fresh pork fat; 750 g lean pork; 750 g pig's liver; 250 g lean veal; 2 spring onions; 1 clove garlic; 75 g butter; 250 g chicken livers; 4 tablespoons brandy; 50 ml double cream; 1½ teaspoons lemon juice; 25 g flour; 1 egg; ½ teaspoon quatre-

épices; 1½ tablespoons salt; pepper; 125 g piece of cooked ox tongue or ham; 250 g fresh pork fat from the back (lard gras); 1 bayleaf.

Mince the fat and lean pork, the pig's liver and the veal and put into a large bowl. Chop the spring onions and mash the garlic with salt. Heat the butter in a frying pan and in it gently soften the onions and garlic. Use a perforated spoon to transfer to the bowl of minced meats. In the fat that remains, gently sauté the chicken livers until they are just firm but still pink inside. Use a perforated spoon to transfer to a separate plate and set aside. Pour the brandy into the pan and deglaze, scraping in any bits from the sides as you do so using a wooden spoon. Pour this liquor on to the meats and add the cream and lemon juice. Add the flour, egg, spices, salt and pepper and mix well. Preheat the oven to regulo 4, 180 °C (350 °F). Cube the tongue or ham and set aside. Cut the fat into thin sheets and use to line the bottom and sides of a 3 l mould. If you wish to do so, it is at this stage that you should test the pâté mixture for seasoning by frying a small spoonful in a frying pan first. (For testing this must be thoroughly cooked since pork should never be eaten raw.) Put half the mixture into the terrine, then arrange the chicken livers and the cubed tongue or ham down the centre. Cover with the rest of the mixture. Place sheets of fat over the top and place the bayleaf on top of that. Cover with foil then with the lid. Place the terrine in a *bain-marie* half-filled with boiling water and set in the middle of the oven for 2 hours or until the juices run clear and are no longer pink. Remove the foil completely. Set the pâté aside to cool. After an hour, place a fresh piece of foil on top and weight down. When the pâté is cool put in the refrigerator still with its weight on top until thoroughly chilled and keep for two or three days to allow the flavour to develop fully.

PÂTÉ DE CHAGNY

A very quick-to-make pâté. The sausage meat provides a convenient form of fresh pork since there is no mincing to be done.

6 rashers green streaky bacon; 250 g chicken livers; 200 g sausage meat; 1 egg; pinch each of thyme, basil and marjoram; seasoning; 1 tablespoon brandy; 2 tablespoons dry sherry; 1 bayleaf.

Pre-heat the oven to regulo 5, 190 °C (375 °F). Remove the rinds and bones from the bacon and use to line the inside of a 1 l pâté dish. Chop the livers finely. If the livers are bought frozen as they so often are you will find it is easier to chop them while they are still frozen; alternatively grate them on the coarse side of the grater. Beat the sausage meat in a large bowl using a wooden spoon, then gradually add the chopped liver. Beat in the egg, the herbs and the seasoning, bearing in mind that there is some seasoning already in the sausage meat. (If you are unsure of the desired amount of seasoning fry a little of the mixture in a tablespoon of oil first to taste, then correct if necessary.) Add the liquor and beat well. Pour the mixture into the lined dish. Lay over the bacon trimmings and the bayleaf. Cover the dish with the lid or tightly with a piece of foil. Set in a *bain-marie* half-filled with boiling water and bake for about an hour or until the juices run clear in colour and are no longer pink. It is impossible to be precise regarding the time it will take to cook since this depends partly on the thickness of the dish and partly on its shape. These are factors to be considered in addition to the accuracy of the oven. Remove from the oven and allow to cool for about an hour. The juices will be absorbed back into the pâté: do not pour them away. Place a weight on the pâté to make it a better shape and firmer for cutting. Keep for several days before eating.

Note You must start to cook the pâté in a *bain-marie* half-filled with boiling water because if cold water is used, this has to heat through before the pate starts to cook and this will extend the cooking time considerably.

CHICKEN LIVER PÂTÉ

Not a baked pâté. It is cooked briefly in a frying pan; the livers are then mixed with butter and brandy, seasoned and simply packed into a little dish until set. It should be pink in colour.

300 g chicken livers; 25 g butter (first amount); 2 tablespoons brandy; 2 tablespoons port; 1 small clove garlic; salt and pepper; thyme; 50 g butter (second amount); dripping.

Remove any greenish and stringy bits from the livers. Melt the butter in a small pan, add the livers whole, and gently sauté for about 4 minutes or until firm but still pink inside. Remove to a wooden board and chop finely or put in a mortar and pound until smooth. Meanwhile add the brandy to the juices remaining in the pan and simmer for a minute or two, scraping in any bits using a wooden spoon. Add the port. Mash the garlic with salt and add this, together with the liquor, additional salt, pepper and thyme, to the chicken livers. Melt the second amount of butter and mix in with the livers. Pack the mixture into a small terrine and allow to set. Melt some clean dripping (pork, goose or duck) and pour over the pâté to a depth of 1 cm and allow to set. The pâté should be kept for several days before eating. It will keep for weeks in the refrigerator provided it has a good layer of fresh and clean dripping sealing it over.

SMOOTH LIVER PÂTÉ

This is a rich yet simple pâté made in the blender. Fine shreds of green pepper make a refreshing garnish.

450 g chicken livers; 4 tablespoons double cream; 2 tablespoons brandy; salt and pepper; Garnish: fine shreds green pepper.

Preheat the oven to regulo 3, 170 °C (325 °F). Remove any stringy bits from the livers and place in the jar of an electric blender together with the cream and brandy. Season with salt and pepper and blend until smooth. If you are unsure of the amount of seasoning, fry a little of the mixture and correct if necessary. Pour the mixture into a well-buttered loaf tin, cover with foil and set in a *bain-marie* half-filled with boiling water. Place in the middle of the oven and bake for 35 minutes or until the juices are no longer pink. Allow to cool for an hour, then gently weight down to give a better shape. Unmould when cold. Serve garnished with shredded green pepper.

RILLETTES

Potted belly pork is available in the United Kingdom only at very high-class delicatessens or at French *charcuteries* and at such high-class establishments as Harrods and Robert Jackson's in London. It is distinguished by its very creamy shred-like texture achieved only by preparing it by hand. On no account must it be put in the blender.

> *600 g belly of pork; 25 g lard; salt and pepper; ½ teaspoon quatre-épices (see p. 36) or other spices according to taste.*

Preheat the oven to regulo ¼, 95 °C (200 °F). Remove the rind and bone from the pork and cut the pork into cubes of about 3 cm. Put into a small but deepish dish with the lard and cover tightly with foil or the lid. Place in the oven and leave for about 8 hours or overnight. Pour off the fat and reserve it. Use two forks, one in each hand to tear the meat apart in shreds — it should be so tender and melting that it almost falls apart. Add to it most of the reserved fat and season with salt and pepper. It can be further seasoned according to taste with *quatre-épices* or with thyme or cloves. Pack the rillettes into small jars to allow to cool. To keep, pour a layer of melted lard over the top to exclude air and keep in a cool place or in the refrigerator. Provided the jar is scrupulously clean, it will keep for months in this way. Rillettes should be served at room temperature, not straight from the refrigerator.

Note The point of cooking the pork in a small but deep dish is to cut down on surface area to discourage evaporation and drying out. On no account must the meat be allowed to brown or to become hardened around the edges.

FROMAGE DE TÊTE (BRAWN)

Shredded or cubed pig's head set in the jelly which is arrived at naturally by reducing the liquid in which it is cooked.

> *½ pig's head; 125 g beef skirt; ½ bottle dry white wine; water; 1 onion; 1 carrot; 10 peppercorns; bouquet garni; lemon juice; nutmeg; salt and pepper.*

Ask the butcher to put the pig's head in the brine tub for a few days if you can afford to wait. As little as one day's brining is sufficient for the saltpetre in the brine to impart a rosy glow to the pork and to improve the flavour. Brining a pig's head can take up to 5 days, in which case the head must be soaked in cold water before cooking to extract the salty taste; this can be done overnight. If you are unsure how salty the pig's head (or indeed any other salted meat) is, you can test and remedy it by putting the pig's head into a large pan, covering with cold water, bringing to the boil then tasting the water to see how much salt there is. If you suspect there is too much, throw away this water, cover with fresh water and repeat the process. The water will once again draw out the salt remaining in the meat through osmotic action. When you are satisfied, proceed with the recipe. Put the pig's head and the beef into a large pan, cover with cold water and bring to the boil. Throw all this water away with the scum (that is, you blanch it) and recover with the wine and more fresh water. Cut the onion and carrot into pieces and add to the pan together with the peppercorns and *bouquet garni.* Bring to the boil then cover the pan tightly with a lid and turn the heat down as low as it will go so that the liquor barely simmers. Leave for 3 to 4 hours or until the meat falls away from the bone. Have two bowls ready and into one of them put the pig's head and the beef. Discard the vegetables and herbs. Reduce the liquor in the pan to about 275 ml over a fast heat without the lid to allow the liquid to evaporate. Meanwhile, when cool enough to handle, remove the meat from the bones, transferring it into the second bowl as you do so. Cut the meats into neat cubes and place in a basin or loaf tin. As the liquor reduces, taste it and as it reaches the amount required, season it with lemon juice, nutmeg, salt and pepper.

Pour this liquor over the meats and put in a cool place to set. To unmould, dip the dish or the tin into another vessel containing hot water to melt sufficient of the jelly inside for it to loosen. This works more quickly on a tin mould than on ceramics or glass. Slightly warmed, toasted breadcrumbs can be pressed into the brawn to serve. Garnish with parsley.

Note Unlike meat and liver pâtés, brawn will not keep, but should be eaten fresh and within a few days of making.

The English raised pie can be compared to the French *pâté en croûte*, although the latter is likely to be far more fanciful, with a play of different meats, textures and colours. The simplest English pork pie, on the other hand, can be filled just with seasoned cubes of belly pork. If bacon is incorporated into the pork mixture it will have more flavour and will impart a pinkish tint from the saltpetre used in the curing process of the bacon.

PÂTÉ DE VEAU ET JAMBON (VEAL-AND-HAM PIE)

250 g fresh lean pork from the shoulder or neck, weighed after trimming; 250 g fresh fat bacon weighed after trimming; pepper; spices to taste; 250 g topside veal; 250 g thinly sliced cooked ham; 275 ml aspic jelly; Pastry: 575 g plain flour; 2 rounded teaspoons salt; 1 rounded tablespoon icing sugar; 250 g lard; 200 ml water.

Use a sharp sturdy knife to scrape the pork and bacon into shreds. Season with pepper and with other spices if wished, or with *quatre-épices* (see p. 40). Mix well. Cut the veal into two or three thin slices. To make the pastry sift the flour, salt and icing sugar into a large mixing bowl. Bring the lard and water to the boil. Make a hollow in the flour and immediately pour in the boiling liquid. Use a wooden spoon to mix and form a paste. When the paste is cool enough, knead by hand until smooth. Meanwhile preheat the oven to regulo 4, 180 °C (350 °F). To form the pie first grease a hinged pie mould or a loose-bottomed cake tin large enough to take the meat. Cut two-thirds off the lump of pastry and place in the middle of the mould. Flatten it with the knuckles and fingers and gradually work it up the sides of the tin until it reaches the rim. Try to make the pastry of even thickness, taking care on the corners, where it tends to form a thick 'wadge'. Starting and finishing with the pork and bacon mixture, layer the meats alternately until all is used up. Using the remaining pastry, roll out to form a lid; damp the edges with water and fix into place. Try to fold the surplus from the sides up and over the lid in traditional style. Trim off any excess as you go. Crimp the edges using the fingers or use a fork. This is not only decorative but also performs the function of thoroughly sealing the two edges of pastry together. Use the trimmings to make pastry leaves or cut-outs. Make a hole in the middle of the crust; this will let out steam and the aspic can be poured through. Decorate this funnel with a pastry tassel (see p. 152). Brush the whole pie crust with beaten egg and place in the middle of the oven. After ½ or ¾ hour, the pie will need covering loosely with greaseproof paper to prevent the pastry from becoming too brown. Bake for 1½ hours altogether. Remove from the oven and allow to cool. Meanwhile prepare the aspic. When the pie is cool and the aspic is also cool but still liquid fill up the pie through the hole in the centre. Should it start to run through the bottom, put the pie in the refrigerator until the aspic sets, then continue gently to fill it up again. Remove the pie from the mould.

Note No salt is added to the meats since the bacon provides this. The aspic may conveniently be made from commercial crystals and flavoured with a little sherry and a squeeze of lemon juice. To be certain of a really crunchy crust top and sides it is possible to remove the pie from the mould before the end of cooking time and place it back in the oven for the final 15 minutes or until done to your liking. The texture of the pie is superior if the meats are cut into shreds with a knife and not simply put through a mincer.

OLIVE PÂTÉ

A plum-coloured pâté, creamy and strong. Its impact on people is varied.

1 onion; 125 g unsalted butter; 175 g black olives; 3 tablespoons double cream, or sour cream or cream cheese; pepper; thyme.

Chop the onion finely and soften gently in the butter over a low heat. Meanwhile pit the olives, then place in the jar of an electric blender together with the onions, butter and cream. Blend until smooth. Season to taste. Pour into ramekins to set.

Note If the olives are difficult to pit, wriggle them one at a time between finger and thumb to loosen the stone from the flesh. The larger olives are often easier to pit than the small ones. Also, do not automatically add salt before tasting as the olives themselves provide this.

TARAMOSALATA

The famous Greek mousse-like blend of olive oil, smoked cod's roe and lemon juice, eaten traditionally with warmed *pitta* bread.

> *1 slice stale white bread; 125 g smoked cod's roe; up to 275 ml olive oil; juice of 1 lemon; pepper; parsley; additional water or lemon juice.*

Remove the crusts from the bread and discard. Soak the bread under a cold running tap, then squeeze thoroughly. Place the bread in a large bowl and, to keep it steady while mixing, stand the bowl on a damp cloth. Mash the bread with a fork then add the cod's roe minus any skin. Blend well. Using a wooden spoon and as if making mayonnaise add the oil alternately with the lemon juice, a few drops at a time to start with, then in ever increasing amounts, stirring constantly. If the mixture seems to curdle, simply add small amounts of water or lemon juice until it becomes creamy. When all the oil is used up, thin further with water or lemon juice. The consistency should be creamy. Season to taste with pepper; you may not need to add salt since the cod's roe provides this. Chop the parsley finely and fold into the mixture. Turn the mixture into a dish and chill. Everyone helps themselves to taramosalata as they please.

Note You will find that recipes for taramosalata vary enormously in the proportion of olive oil to fish roe used. This recipe is for the average English palate, although a more bland oil than olive oil may be preferred. For Greek tastes cut the amount of oil down to about two or three tablespoons, include plenty of lemon juice and serve with large quantities of wine. Taramosalata should be made with the smoked roe of the grey mullet but this is difficult to acquire and smoked cod's roe is usually used instead.

Depending on the texture you prefer, this hand-made taramosalata can be made smoother by adding a little extra water and using an electric blender.

SMOKED MACKEREL PÂTÉ

Uncooked. A simple blend of shredded smoked fish and thick cream seasoned with salt, pepper and lemon juice. It is easy to prepare by hand.

½ smoked mackerel; 200 to 300 ml double cream; salt and white pepper; lemon juice.

A mackerel smoked whole is moister and easier to work than the boned and smoked fillets. Remove the skin, bones and blackish bits from the fish. Place in a bowl and flake with a fork. In another bowl, whip the cream until it is thick but still glossy. Use a plastic spatula to fold the cream into the fish. If you beat it the cream will curdle and the mixture will become watery. Season to taste with salt and white pepper and lemon juice. Spoon the mixture into a small bowl, smooth over and use the point of a sharp knife to decorate as you please. Chill well before serving.

Note Of all the smoked fish pâtés, mackerel is particularly easy to make by hand because of its soft fatty flesh, and the bones are easy to remove. White pepper is used in creamy coloured mixtures such as this and in white sauces. White pepper is simply black peppercorns with the skin removed. This pâté would be well presented in a brightly coloured or a dark dish.

Pâté is traditionally served with crusty bread or Melba toast. With most pâtés there should be no need to serve butter because the pâté itself should be creamy enough, but this is essentially a matter of taste.

MELBA TOAST

Thin crunchy curls of toasted bread.

Large thin slices of commercial bread work well for this; they should be several days old. The reason for starting with stale bread is that with new bread ridges form when you split it, which spoils the effect when it is toasted on the second side. If you have never made Melba toast you may think it is impossible for thin toast to be split into two, but try it! It is easier than it seems.

Put the bread on the grill pan at a medium distance from the heat and set at a moderate temperature; do not use the electric toaster. Toast both sides of the bread until pale gold. Remove it to a work surface, trim the crusts off, and with a sharp and thin bladed knife gently split the toast into two so that each piece now has an untoasted surface. Lay it flat on the table, hold it down with one hand and slice through with the knife in the other. Return the toast to the grill and gently brown the other sides. It will curl gently. If you toast too fast, however, the corners will burn before the middle is brown. Melba toast keeps crisp for many days so can be prepared well in advance.

5

Fish

Fish is cooked to make it palatable, not to make it tender. It is grilled or fried or baked *en papillote* for quite different reasons from those dictating a decision to grill, fry or bake a piece of meat. Fish does not have the tough connective tissue or the strong elastin that meat has, and so there is a different problem to be overcome: how best to deal with fish — whether filleted, whole or sliced — without overcooking it or allowing it to fall apart. The texture matters a lot because if the fish is fine and firm, it can be sautéed or grilled without falling apart when turned over with a spatula or when being temporarily removed from the pan while the sauce is being made. If, on the other hand, the texture is not fine and firm the fish tends to fall apart, and a more suitable method of cooking is to poach the fish and to make a sauce with the fish remaining in the pan to avoid the risk of breaking the fish when moved. An even safer method is to place the fish on a buttered plate and steam it so that it does not have to be moved about at all during the cooking. Even fish which is fine and firm will fall apart if overcooked because the curd-like substance between the flakes which holds it together will disappear, thus causing the flakes to separate.

Fish is usually divided into three categories: *white*, *oily* and *shell* fish. It is useful to understand that the fat of oily fish is distributed throughout the flesh and this is why salmon, herrings and mackerel are both darker in colour and have more flavour than many others like cod, whiting, plaice and sole. These come into the category of white fish, in which all the fat is contained in the liver leaving the flesh dry, flaky and with little flavour. White fish therefore needs cooking in a way that will make it more tasty, such as frying or barbecuing, or it can be served with a piquant sauce like anchovy, caper or tartare. Flavour can be introduced into the fish itself by marinating it in wine, oil and herbs before cooking. A popular and interesting way of using white fish which might otherwise be dull is to stuff two fillets together like a sandwich with mushrooms, onions and bacon, then to mask with a light cheese sauce and bake in the oven until the top is crisp and golden (see p. 55). Another way in which white fish can be prepared is as for *cod au poivre* (see p. 54), which is delicious and has a most exciting taste.

The third category of fish — shellfish — is further divided into molluscs (mussels, cockles) and crustaceans (lobster, crab). These have to be boiled as soon as they are caught because they deteriorate so rapidly. One exception is oysters which, if cooked, become hard so must be eaten raw or heated through only. Shellfish are difficult to digest.

Fish by itself is not as stimulating as meat because it does not contain as many extractives, which are the things that excite the appetite. For this reason it is not usually served as the main course of a meal, except perhaps in summer when light food is required. White fish and oily fish are a very digestible form of protein and are therefore good for invalids. Oily fish is more nutritious than white, the fat-soluble vitamins A and D being contained throughout the flesh. It is also a good source of iodine.

Ideally all fish should be cooked and eaten soon after it is caught because it deteriorates rapidly. Use the day it is bought if possible. Look out for the following in fresh fish: bright prominent eyes, firm flesh, a pleasant smell, plenty of scales, and red gills (these are the breathing organs of the fish and if they are still red it shows that oxygen has been breathed in recently). When you get the fish home, wash it, put it on a plate and cover with a cloth wrung out in vinegar water. Keep it in the refrigerator. Shellfish are difficult to open when fresh because the muscles have not had time to deteriorate.

Although the fishmonger will prepare the fish as you want by scaling, cleaning, filleting and skinning, ask him if he will allow you to watch so that next time you can prepare the fish yourself if you wish to.

To skin fish, lay the fish skin side down (figure 5.1).

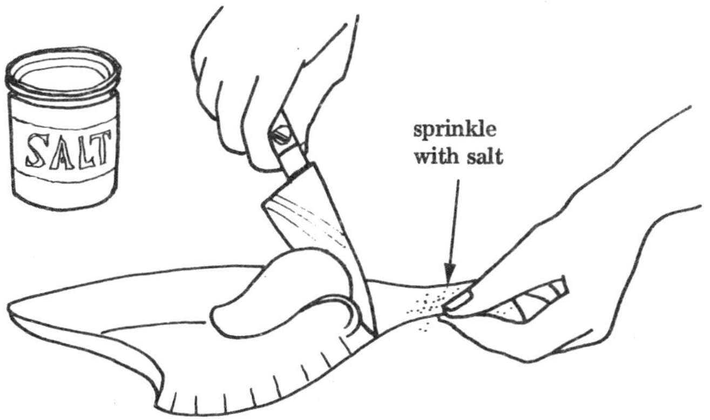

Figure 5.1 Skinning a fish

Sprinkle the tail with salt: this ensures a firm grip. Grasp the tail in the left hand and use a well-sharpened knife in the right to cut the flesh from the skin. The knife should be held almost flat with the table and you will have to pull the tail end taught as you cut in a sawing motion.

Watching an expert is far better than trying to learn by reading about it, however. Scaling is done by holding the tail end — with salt on your fingers if it is very slippery — and using the back of a knife held in the other hand to scrape down towards the head of the fish. Wash in clean water. To clean round fish (herring, mackerel, trout) slit from the throat to one-third of the way down the body, making sure not to slit the internal organs, and remove them with two fingers. Remove any blackish traces that remain with salt and rinse under running water. To clean flat fish (plaice, sole) in which the belly is just under the head remove the gills and cut a small opening. Remove the internal organs. Rinse well.

Notes on the various methods of cooking fish follow. Some methods lend themselves to endless variation, especially poaching, and baking stuffed fish, whereas steaming and deep-fat frying are fairly straightforward methods that suggest a simple garnish of lemon and parsley or serving with a separate sauce such as hollandaise or mayonnaise.

Fish *bouillon* and fish *fumet* are liquors used to boil or braise and to poach fish respectively. The basic difference is in the concentration of flavours (see below and p. 59).

A *velouté* sauce when applied to fish is made by combining a white *roux* with a reduced *fumet.* It is one of the great basic sauces (see p. 51).

Recipes for making a *bouillon*, a *fumet* and a fish *velouté* sauce follow.

Herbs considered to go well with fish are tarragon, dill, basil, parsley, rosemary, fennel and thyme.

Fish dishes should either be served alone, or simply with boiled potatoes or fresh white bread. A salad or other vegetable can be served separately *after* the fish course.

POACHED FISH

Small pieces of fish half covered with the chosen liquor cooked either in the oven with a piece of buttered paper on top, or in a flameproof casserole, basting frequently. The sauce is derived from the cooking liquor.

Fish can be cooked in red wine, white wine, sherry, vermouth (see recipe on p. 52), port, milk, water or in a fish *fumet*. A fish *fumet* is like a concentrated fish *bouillon*. After the fish has been poached it is removed to a heated serving dish while the liquor is reduced and finished in any one of a large number of ways to make a sauce. The simplest way is to stir in a cream and egg yolk liaison, season to taste, just cover the fish — called masking — and serve. Poaching takes between 7 and 10 minutes in the oven set at regulo 4, 180 °C (350 °F). Foil should never be used to cover the dish because of the reaction between the aluminium and the acid in the wine or lemon juice.

FISH FUMET

See above. This is a white wine fish stock used to poach fish. The *fumet* is reduced to concentrate the flavours and is made into a sauce when the fish is cooked and has been removed.

Combined with a *blond roux* a *fumet* becomes a fish *velouté* sauce — one of the basic white sauces from which there are many derivatives. A *roux* is a cooked butter and flour liaison used for thickening liquids in the making of sauces. A *blond roux* is one that has not been allowed to brown.

1 kg fish heads, bones and skin; 275 ml white wine or 200 ml vermouth; 1 onion; 1 bayleaf; a few parsley stems; 1 teaspoon lemon juice; a few mushroom stems; salt; sprig of thyme.

Chop up the fish trimmings and put in a pan with the liquor. Bring to the boil. Cut up the onion and add together with all the other ingredients. Simmer for 30 minutes and strain immediately.

Note The leaves of parsley and the caps of mushrooms tend to darken the liquor, which is why the stems only are used. Do not cook the *fumet* for longer than 30 minutes before straining, otherwise it will become bitter.

An ideal fish for poaching is sole since its firm close-textured flesh does not fall apart during cooking. It can be removed from the dish while the sauce is being made without any harm. This applies also to brill, John Dory and turbot.

VELOUTÉ SAUCE

A white stock thickened with a *blond roux*. In this case, fish stock is used although a *velouté* can be made with chicken, vegetable or veal.

275 ml fish fumet; Roux; 25 g butter; 25 g flour; salt and pepper.

The *fumet* should be sufficiently concentrated in flavour, so taste it first. Melt the butter gently in a medium sized saucepan, add the flour and cook the *roux* without browning, for 2 to 3 minutes, stirring constantly with a wooden spoon. Remove from the heat and add the *fumet*, a little at a time to begin with, then in ever-increasing amounts, stirring well between each addition and the next using a wooden spoon. You should now have a lump-free thin sauce. Return it once more to a moderate heat and bring to the boil, stirring all the time, when it will thicken. Season to taste. Use this sauce to mask the fish.

Lemon sole and other fish that tend to flake apart during cooking respond well to poaching in the way described for sole vermouth below. A shallow oven-to-table flameproof dish is required. The fish is poached, then sauced and served all in the same dish; since the fish does not have to be lifted there is no risk of breaking it. The cooking liquor, in this case vermouth, must be concentrated enough before the fish is put into it for the finished sauce to have the right amount of flavour.

SOLE VERMOUTH

Fillets of lemon sole poached in vermouth, tinted pink with tomato and finished with cream.

> *275 ml dry white vermouth; 25 g butter; 2 teaspoons tomato purée; 8 fillets lemon sole; 200 ml double cream; 25 g butter (second amount); salt and pepper; Extra thickening (optional): 1 egg yolk; 1 teaspoon flour.*

The flameproof dish which is needed here should be just big enough for the fish to sit comfortably in four pairs side by side. If it is too big the sauce will dry out round the edges.

Pour the vermouth into the dish and set over a moderate heat. Bring to the boil, then turn down to simmer. Reduce the amount of vermouth to two-thirds. Add the first amount of butter and the tomato purée. Lay pairs of fillets side by side in the liquor and gently spoon the liquid over the fish as it poaches. This should take about 3 minutes. If a thin sauce is required pour the cream into the liquid in a steady stream, let it bubble, then stir in the second amount of butter off the heat. Season to taste. If a thicker sauce is preferred, first combine the cream, egg yolk and flour, then add to the liquor in a thin stream, stirring constantly. Allow to bubble and thicken, then stir in the second amount of butter off the heat. Season to taste and serve.

Note Adding a small amount of butter to a sauce after it is cooked makes it more glossy.

SAUTÉED FISH

Shallow frying. The simplest way is to dip the fish in milk, then in flour, breadcrumbs or oatmeal, and fry both sides in butter. It is suitable for small whole fish, fillets and slices of larger fish.

Choice of fish; milk; flour or breadcrumbs; equal quantities of butter and oil; salt; Garnish: lemon wedges; parsley sprigs.

Dip both sides of the fish in a saucer of milk, then on to a plate of breadcrumbs or flour. Heat the butter and oil gently in a suitable sized pan for the amount of fish you have to allow the fillets to sit side by side in pairs. The fat in the pan must be hot and foamy before the fish is put in, otherwise the breadcrumbs will absorb it and become soggy or fall off. The fish should be sautéed over a medium heat that is not too hot or the skin, if any, will become tough. The time will be between 3 and 8 minutes, depending on the thickness of the fish and it should be carefully turned once to lightly brown both sides. Lightly salt the fish, then arrange on a hot dish and garnish with lemon wedges and parsley. Pour the frying butter over it and serve.

Note Oatmeal is often used with trout instead of breadcrumbs and flour.

A more stylish way of presenting sautéed fish is the recipe that follows.

COD AU POIVRE

A sauté. Fish fillets or steaks heavily encrusted with crushed peppercorns and flour, sautéed in butter, flamed with brandy, the pan juices deglazed with port and finished with thick cream.

> *4 cod steaks, 2½ cm thick, or 4 fillets; salt; 3 heaped tablespoons black peppercorns; 1 rounded dessertspoon flour; 2 tablespoons oil; 125 g butter; 60 ml brandy; 60 ml port; 125 ml chicken or light veal stock; 150 ml double cream.*

Trim the steaks and skewer the open ends if necessary, or skin the fillets and fold in three, skin-side inside. Season the fish with salt. Crush the peppercorns in a pestle and mortar, or by using the back of a teaspoon on a hard board. (On no account put them in an electric grinder even for a few seconds as this makes a certain amount of powder which spoils the final effect.) Mix them with the flour on a plate and press the fish into the flour and pepper mixture, coating the fish on both sides. Heat the oil in a large frying pan, then add half the butter only. When it foams and is hot, add the pieces of fish. Allow to cook at a high temperature for a second or two, then lower the heat a little and continue cooking for about 2 minutes. Carefully turn the fish over with a spatula and do the other side. Pour the brandy over the fish and tip to one side so that the flame ignites it. When the flames have subsided, remove the fish and arrange on a heated serving dish. Keep it warm. Add the port to the pan juices and deglaze, using a wooden spoon to scrape the tasty bits from inside the pan. Pour in the stock and reduce until thick and syrupy. Stir in the cream and then the remaining butter, cut in pieces. Mask the fish with some of the sauce. Serve the rest separately.

BAKED FISH

The simplest way to bake fish is to place it in a buttered dish, season, cover with buttered paper and bake until done. It is a suitable method for cooking most fish, large and small, whole, fillets or slices, stuffed or plain, with or without a sauce. A whole fish is often trussed into a curve to simulate swimming.

White fish that has little flavour is more interesting if baked with a stuffing as in the following recipe.

BAKED STUFFED COD

Fillets or slices. Onions, bacon and mushrooms make the tasty stuffing. The fish arranged in an oven-to-table dish is masked with a cheese sauce and baked in the oven until golden.

> *4 matching pieces of cod fillet or slices; 1 large onion; 4 rashers streaky bacon; 250 g mushrooms; 25 g butter; pepper; For the sauce: 25 g butter; 25 g flour; 275 ml milk; 50 g Cheddar cheese; salt and pepper; For the topping: 25 g butter; 2 handfuls fresh white breadcrumbs.*

When using slices of cod, remove the bones. Set aside. Chop the onion, bacon and mushrooms finely, then melt the butter carefully in a frying pan and gently soften them. Season with pepper. When cool enough to handle, use to stuff the fish. When using fillets, they can be sandwiched in pairs or the fillets can be rolled up individually, turban style, skin side inside with the stuffing in the middle.

When using slices of cod, put the stuffing in the space occupied by the bone. Arrange in an oven-to-table dish and set aside while you make the sauce. Melt the butter carefully in a medium sized saucepan, stir in the flour and cook without browning for several minutes, stirring with a wooden spoon. Remove the pan from the heat. Add the milk a little at a time to start with, stirring well between each addition and the next until it is all used up. You should now have a lump-free but thin sauce. Return it to a medium heat and stir constantly until the sauce thickens and comes to the directly into it. Beat the sauce until the cheese melts—off the heat. Season to taste with salt and pepper. Mask the fish with this sauce. Make the topping by melting the butter carefully in a frying pan and, when it is hot and foamy, toss in the breadcrumbs. Fry them until a pale gold, stirring or tossing them in the pan to keep an even colour. Scatter them over the fish. Preheat the oven at regulo 5, 190 °C (375 °F). Bake until golden brown for 35 to 40 minutes.

Note The time taken to bake fish depends on its thickness or, as in this case, whether the fish is stuffed. This increases the time required. When baking fish plain, you can tell whether it is cooked or not by the appearance. It should have a white curd-like substance between the flakes and be quite opaque. Cooked fish also flakes easily from the bone.

DEEP-FRIED FISH

Suitable method for whole flat fish or fillets such as sole, plaice or turbot. The prepared fish is fried at 183 °C (360 °F) and when it rises to the surface, showing that it is done, it is simply removed on to kitchen paper to drain, then served on a heated plate and garnished with parsley and lemon.

Prepare the fish in one of the following ways. Dip in milk then dust with flour, shaking off the excess, or dip in egg and breadcrumbs, or dip in batter (see recipe below). Do not add too many fish at once, otherwise the temperature of the oil will be reduced, the oil will be absorbed by the fish and the fish will become soggy. The fish should come out crisp. It is wise to use a cooking thermometer.

BATTER FOR DEEP-FRYING FISH

125 g flour; 3 tablespoons oil; 150 ml water; pinch of salt; 1 egg white.

Mix the flour and oil in a basin, then gradually beat in the water. Add the salt. Leave to stand for several hours before using, and finally beat in the beaten white of an egg to lighten.

GRILLED FISH

For whole small fish and fish slices.

If the chosen fish has thick flesh, score it to allow the heat to penetrate right through. Dust the fish with flour, then brush liberally with oil to prevent it sticking to the grill pan or the hinged fish grill if that is used. Small pieces should be cooked faster than thicker ones but not too fast, otherwise the skin will become dry and tough. Start cooking under a preheated grill. Turn the fish once, allowing 2 to 3 minutes for each side. Garnish with lemon and parsley and serve a herb or other kind of butter separately.

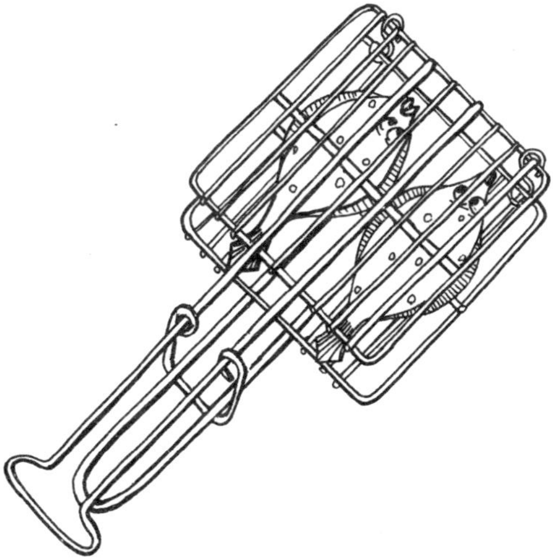

Figure 5.2 A hinged fish grill

A hinged fish grill (figure 5.2) enables you to turn fish cooking under a grill or over a barbecue without disturbing it.

There is less chance that the fish will break up done in this way than if it were turned with a spatula.

BARBECUED FISH

Oily fish such as a whole mackerel is particularly suited because it remains moist during cooking. The same applies to grilled fish. Prepare in the same way as for grilled fish, remembering to oil the grid. Calculate the cooking time at 15 minutes per 500 g.

FISH COOKED EN PAPILLOTE

A conservative method of treating fish whereby it is wrapped in paper or foil and baked in the oven. The simplest way is to add a knob of butter, season and wrap in such a way that the juices are retained when served. Calculate approximately 20 minutes per 500 g at regulo 3, 170 °C (325 °F).

STEAMED FISH

A good conservative method of cooking fish that retains flavour and nutrients, and is also good for allowing the fish to hold its shape.

Prepare the fish in any of the following ways. Either prepare as *en papillote* (that is, season, add a knob of butter and wrap in buttered paper or foil) and steam in a steamer; or, lay the fish on a plate, sprinkle with lemon, season, cover with another plate and stand it on top of a pan of boiling water. The third method is to lay the fish in a dish, sprinkle with lemon, season, cover the dish and set in a *bain-marie.* Cook in the oven. Test whether it is done by the appearance — the fish should have a white curd-like substance between the flakes. The time taken to cook is 10 to 15 minutes.

BRAISED FISH

Good for large fish and large pieces. The fish is simply laid in an ovenproof dish, covered with a *court-bouillon* (see below), then covered with buttered greaseproof paper and set in the oven at regulo 3, 170 °C (325 °F). The time taken to cook is 10 minutes for a thick fish weighing 1 kg or 7 minutes if the fish is a thin one.

If wished, the fish can be first laid on a thin layer of onions and carrots that have first been softened by heating in butter before the liquor is added. The fish should never be covered with aluminium foil because this would react with the acid from the wine, vinegar or lemon in the *court-bouillon.* The cooking liquor from braised fish is ultimately reduced until concentrated and used to make the sauce or it can be added to the sauce.

BOILED FISH

The fish is not actually boiled but is simmered in a *court-bouillon.* This method has limited use for everyday purposes because it is suitable only for large whole fish such as salmon and salmon trout.

> *1 whole cleaned fish, weighed; For court-bouillon: 1 kg fish heads, bones and skin; 2 l water; 1 l dry white wine; 100 ml white vinegar; 2 onions; 2 carrots; 2 sticks celery; 50 g butter; 5 to 6 stems parsley; 2 bayleaves; sprig thyme; salt; 10 peppercorns.*

Calculate the time for cooking the fish at 8 minutes per 500 g plus an additional 5 minutes. If the fish is to be cooked in a fish kettle, lay it on the trivet. If it is to be cooked in a pan, tie it up with muslin. Mash up the fish trimmings and place in a large pan with the liquids and bring to the boil. Meanwhile, chop the onions, carrots and celery roughly and soften in the butter without browning. Skim the liquid as the froth rises to the surface. Add the vegetables, parsley, bay, thyme, salt and peppercorns and simmer, partially covered, for 30 minutes, skimming from time to time. Discard the fish trimmings and aromatics and strain the *court-bouillon* through a double thickness of muslin into the pan in which the whole fish is to be cooked. Lower the fish into the *court-bouillon*, adding more water if needed to cover. Bring slowly to the boil, then turn the heat down so low that the liquid barely simmers. Cook for the required length of time, then remove the pan from the heat and allow the fish to cool in its poaching liquid. Carefully remove the fish and treat according to the particular recipe you are following. The stock can be used to make the aspic coating if it is to be a more elaborate presentation—otherwise it can be made into a fish soup to be served another time.

Note A fish stock should never be cooked for more than 30 minutes before the fish trimmings are removed, otherwise it will be bitter. The wine and vinegar (or lemon juice) in the *court-bouillon* helps to cook the fish and prevents it flaking apart. A more concentrated form of *court-bouillon* is called a fish *fumet* and is used for poaching fish, after which the liquor is reduced and made into the accompanying sauce.

6

A Roast Beef Dinner

Practical experience in producing this kind of meal counts very much towards its success. A cook may have a wide culinary repertoire and cook individual dishes well, but still fail on this occasion. It is a good exercise in time and motion which should result in the meat being perfect, the vegetables ready not a minute too soon, the gravy made, in addition to having the table set and the diners assembled. The pace quickens fast — it is just before serving that everything seems to be happening at once amidst clattering saucepan lids, steam and delicious smells. A typical menu consists of roast fore-rib of beef, Yorkshire pudding, gravy, horseradish sauce, roast potatoes, sprouts, cauliflower, mustard, to be followed by a fruit pie and cream. The importance of choosing the right cut of good quality beef is paramount. For this, the customer takes a lot on trust from the butcher, because although the cut is identifiable, the quality is not so easily determined simply by looking at it. How can we tell if the meat came from an animal bred purely for beef and not from a milk cow or a stud bull? The best meat comes ideally from male animals castrated young, grass-fed and from 5 to 6 years old. These are oxen or bullocks or steers — all of which imply the same meaning. Good quality beef can also come from heifers, which are cows that have not calved. Meat for roasting should have plenty of fat around it with marbling or specks of fat within the lean itself. Many people misguidedly look for very lean roasting joints not realising that fat gives flavour and helps keep the meat moist while it cooks. The fat marbled inside the lean bastes the joint from within. The hanging of beef, the butcher's responsibility, is also a great contributory factor to its tenderness and flavour. Beef hung for 3 weeks is ideal but it will be expensive — the butcher has to have the space and has to make up for the loss of weight incurred by increasing the price. Well hung meat is drier than fresh and darker in colour. The flavour is superior.

Roasting meat as we understand it should really be called baking since the food is cooked in an oven uncovered without any liquid added. True roasting is done before an open fire. However, it is a cooking method suitable only for the most tender cuts. The most tender of these tender cuts — sirloin, fillet and wing-rib — are suitable for roasting in a fairly fast (hot) oven. The high temperature does not make them tough. Fore-rib, back-rib and top-rib, on the other hand, should be roasted more slowly in a moderate oven so that they are tender on the inside by the time the outside is done. Any meat on the bone can be removed and then rolled into a compact joint and tied with string before roasting, and this helps to keep it moist and makes carving easy. The choice is a matter of personal preference, although it is more aesthetically pleasing to see the meat on the bone, apart from which it is good to have a bone to gnaw at cold the following day.

If it is to be stored for a day or two fresh meat should be completely removed from its wrapping, laid on a plate and placed on the bottom shelf of the refrigerator or in a cool place. Meat stored in polythene quickly turns sour.

The time taken to roast a piece of beef is partly assessed by weighing it and allowing so many minutes per 500 g. However, a 3 kg rib that has a large flat cut surface will cook more quickly than the same joint boned and rolled and thus made into a solid compact mass that takes longer for the heat to penetrate. The cooking time will also depend on the make of oven used — there are often enormous differences between them. The theoretical roasting charts found in most cookery books should be regarded as a helpful guide only, bearing in mind these remarks. If you are a beginner, it would be a help to invest in a meat cooking thermometer. This is inserted into the centre of the meat while the dial tells you whether the meat is rare, medium or well done and gives readings not only for beef but also for pork, lamb and poultry. When you have roasted meat a few times you will notice the signs that tell you how much or whether the meat is done. A well-done roast will be brown on the outside and will also have given off a large amount of drippings that you will hear sizzling loudly in the pan. An underdone joint will have few drippings as the juices are contained within the meat itself. You cannot therefore have rare beef and a lot of drippings as well. One further factor that affects the time taken to roast a joint is whether or not it was allowed to come to room temperature before being placed in the oven. If meat starts off refrigerator-cold it will take longer.

Some cooks like to sear the meat initially, defined as quickly browning the outside and sealing in the juices. This coagulates and hardens the protein on the outer surface, but must not be carried out for more than 15 minutes otherwise the inside will also start to toughen and the protein fibres will shrink into bundles. I have said that the cooking time depends on several factors and the following is to be used as a basic guide. Meat to be seared should be placed in a preheated regulo 8, 230 °C (450 °F) oven, turning it down to regulo 5, 190 °C (375 °F) for the remainder of the cooking time. Allow 15 minutes per 500 g plus 15 minutes over. Meat can be roasted at a moderate temperature all through, omitting the searing process, however. This is done by placing it in a preheated regulo 5, 190 °C (375 °F) oven allowing 25 minutes per 500 g or 30 minutes if boned and rolled. For the less tender roasting joints (back rib and top rib) it is preferable to cook in a slower oven preheated to regulo 4, 180 °C (350 °F) allowing 40 to 45 minutes per 500 g. All meat to be roasted should be placed on a rack that stands inside the roasting tin. This lifts it out of the juices, allowing it to bake properly all round and not just on the top.

The Yorkshire pudding which traditionally accompanies roast beef was at one time baked in the roasting tin underneath the meat while the meat was cooking. Done in this way the pudding is very tasty, but care has to be taken not to make it too fatty and indigestible. In the north of England another variation was to serve Yorkshire pudding as a separate course before the meat to fill people up so that they would not be able to eat so much meat afterwards. It could be served with gravy or alternatively with golden syrup which the children liked. The most usual way to cook Yorkshire pudding these days is in a separate pan either as one large pudding or as individual puddings. Suffficient fat to cover the base of the Yorkshire pudding pan with a thin film is poured in and is made very hot before the batter is added. It will sizzle. The puddings are then baked at the top of a very hot oven.

The gravy has to be made from the pan drippings towards the end of the meat roasting time. The fat should be removed from the drippings by pouring it off into a clean cup and it should be put aside to use later for something else. The brown meaty bits that remain should be deglazed with a little sherry or port or wine in the roasting tin itself, over the fire, seasoned, then served in a little jug, strained if you wish. Done in this way it would be described as *jus* rather than gravy. To make gravy, the drippings are thickened with either flour or cornflour and stock is added. It is then seasoned and can be strained or left as it is—just as you prefer.

Grated horseradish or horseradish sauce is one of the traditional accompaniments, although fresh horseradish is not always readily available. A little thick fresh cream stirred into the commercial product will greatly improve it.

A small joint or one that is to be cooked rare will not take very long to cook. In this case, the potatoes will not be done in time if cooked from raw and it would be best to parboil them first before putting them in the roasting tin alongside the meat. In addition, it would help if they were cut smaller and were all the same size, to ensure even cooking.

Any number of vegetables of almost any kind accompany beef well, but you may prefer to keep things simple with only one or two kinds. Sprouts should be cooked in an uncovered pan in a minimum of boiling salted water, bearing in mind that the reasons for this include preserving the green colour and preserving vitamin C; they should be boiled for the barest amount of time so that they are cooked but retain their crispness and attractive flavour. If cooked for too long, the taste becomes powerful (see p. 97). Cauliflower can be steamed or boiled and, as with sprouts, the cooking time should be kept to a minimum. It also becomes overstrong the longer it is cooked. Refer to your recipe book for cooking times.

The time plan for producing a roast dinner must start by calculating how long the meat will take to cook and getting it into the oven accordingly. The meat and potatoes will take the longest so these should be prepared first and put to cook. The potatoes can be put alongside the meat or can be cooked in a separate pan. Follow this by setting the table with the condiments, the mustard, horseradish, serving spoons and a long and very thin sharp knife for carving. Also include the side plates and cutlery. Polish the glasses and set these in place also. The Yorkshire pudding batter can then be prepared and allowed to stand until it is time to cook it. Approximately every 20 to 25 minutes baste the meat with its own drippings and turn the potatoes to brown the other sides. Three-quarters-of-an-hour before the meal is to be served, clean and prepare the vegetables. They should not be done much earlier than this because they deteriorate. About half-an-hour before the meal put the meat into the bottom part of the oven, turning the temperature up in order to cook the Yorkshire puddings. (The bottom part of the oven is cooler than the top, so the meat will not spoil when you do this.) Alternatively, if the meat is cooked it can be removed completely from the oven at this stage in order to relax it before it is carved. It makes carving much easier. The Yorkshire puddings take about 25 minutes to cook. Put the dinner plates and serving dishes to warm. Put the hot water on for the vegetables. Cook the vegetables. Make the gravy. Serve.

The fruit pie, which will have been made in advance, can now be placed in the oven to warm through while the main part of the meal is being eaten. It will take about half-an-hour at regulo 3, 170 °C (325 °F).

Following the meal, any juices that have accumulated from the meat should be spooned up and saved for the following day. They could be added to the fat drippings if you like to eat bread and dripping, or, if you plan on making a *rechauffé* dish with the leftover cold meat, they should be included in this.

7

Coq au Vin and other casseroles

The word casserole describes both the food and the container in which it is cooked; the container can be glazed earthenware, stoneware or toughened glass and, if made of copper, stainless steel or enamelled cast iron can be used both on top of the fire in direct contact with the heat source as well as in the oven. The casserole should have a heavy well-fitting lid to prevent evaporation which may also be shaped to cause the condensing steam to fall back on the food being cooked. In the past these pots, which stood by the edge of an open fire, had lids shaped to hold hot coals to speed up cooking from the top.

Casseroles and stews have evolved throughout the world out of one basic necessity — to make tough meat palatable. Casseroling involves cooking the food for a long time, slowly over a low fire or in the oven, and in a liquid. The liquid can be water, stock, wine, cider or beer. Unless a particular recipe is being followed a cook will use whatever liquid happens to be available or most plentiful at the time, provided of course that it is suitable. Thus from wine-growing areas came *coq au vin* and *boeuf bourguignonne;* from the beer-loving Belgians came *carbonnade flamande;* while pork cooked in cider is associated with the English west country, where cider apples grow in abundance.

All animals, whether reared specially for their flesh or not, have both tender and tough meat on the same carcase. Around the legs and neck where the muscles have performed the most work is the meat for casseroling, while around the ribs — not a mobile part — are the cuts and joints for brief grilling, frying or quick roasting. These tender cuts are few and are always most expensive — especially fillet steak. Thus it would be false economy to try to grill or fry 'stewing' meat, and it would be wasteful to use expensive cuts in a casserole. Moreover, the strong muscles of any animal have plenty of flavour, as does meat from an older beast, which is an advantage in a casserole. Consider how bland the flavour of a young animal is, and notice that most veal dishes need to include a strong additional flavour. These basic points apply to all animals and birds, but not to fish.

It has been said that 'a stew is the result of giving casserole ingredients to a thoroughly inexperienced cook'. One may ask what the difference is anyway. The word 'stew' may suggest a pale watery potful of equally pale meat making up perhaps an Irish stew, while a 'casserole' makes one think of succulent cubes of browned meat in a rich tasty sauce. Most home cooks in the United Kingdom have started to give more attention to the initial preparation of the meat and vegetables for casseroling. The simplest way is just to layer the raw meat and common vegetables in the pot, cover with water or stock, season perhaps only with salt and pepper, and then cook it. Alternatively, the meat and vegetables can be browned in fat, the liquid thickened carefully and, with the inclusion of other interesting imported vegetables and spices, infinite blends of flavour and colour can be achieved. But the words stew and casserole, together with the terms braise, fricassée, cooking *à la poêle*, cooking *à l'étuvée* and potroasting are in fact synonymous terms for a method of cooking. The method is described in detail below, using as an example recipe *carbonnade flamande*. Simply stated, it is the cooking of tougher meat slowly in a liquid, and it can have a few or many additional ingredients.

The main ingredients for *carbonnade flamande* are beef, onions and beer. The meat is cut into 1 cm strips about 7 cm long, then it is *sealed*, *browned* or *sautéed* in very hot fat in a large heavy saucepan. The directions to seal, to brown and to sauté mean the same in this context and all these words are commonly used in recipe books. This process is performed for two reasons. One is to seal the juices of the meat *in*; the other is to brown the meat. The degree of brown-ness determines the colour of the drippings, and thus the finished sauce. It is better to induce colour in this way than to employ the use of commercial gravy brownings. This process is best performed in a heavy-bottomed saucepan, which will conduct the heat evenly and minimise the risk of burning. The browning process is done in very hot fat, which has a searing effect; it must not be hot enough to produce smoke and acrid fumes, however. The fat used can be butter, margarine, vegetable oil, lard, clean dripping or a combination of these fats. Oil has the highest smoking point, while butter requires much care when used for this purpose since it burns at a low temperature. A recipe may tell you to use a combination of butter and oil to gain the advantages of both fats, butter having flavour and a generous browning effect and oil a high smoking point. Whatever fat is used, it must be made hot first, then a little of the dry meat is tossed in, in a roomy single layer. It should make a hissing sound. The meat should then be tossed around to brown all sides. This is more easily done with a wooden spoon (although expert chefs toss the meat deftly over and over just by shaking the pan). The meat should then have stiffened and be a rich brown on all sides. It is a process which requires constant attention, and it is important also to remember not to crowd the meat in several layers in a small pan. This would encourage the meat to become wet and steamy and it would start to stew in its own juice. If you have a large amount of meat to prepare do just a little at a time, removing the browned meat on to a plate while you prepare the next batch. The amount of fat is usually stated in the recipe—in effect enough to cover the bottom of the pan with a thin film. The kind of fat may also be stated, but usually it is allright to use whatever you have available. If the recipe states oil but you have a cupful of fresh dripping in your refrigerator, use that. Another important point is to make sure that the meat is dry, otherwise a lot of fat will spit from the pan and the meat will not brown properly. Browning takes approximately 2 to 4 minutes.

Having browned and removed the meat, the next step is to add a little more fat or oil to the pan (in which there are now drippings from the meat) and soften the onions. Stir the onions as you do this over a moderate heat until they become a golden brown, scraping the meaty bits from the bottom of the pan as you do so. Done in this way, onions acquire a distinctive sweetness as the natural sugar present in all onions turns to caramel. When using garlic in this recipe avoid frying in hot fat without the presence of some other moist ingredient such as onions since garlic contains little moisture of its own and burns easily without due care.

Now all the meat is returned to the pan with the onions and garlic. Add the beer, bayleaf, herbs, vinegar, sugar, salt and pepper. Bring to just under the boil, stirring occasionally, then reduce the heat to minimum, put on a tight-fitting lid and cook for 1½ to 2 hours (the time will depend on the quality of the meat, which can be tested by chewing a piece or by piercing it with a sharp knife). The liquid must never be allowed to boil since this toughens the meat; the surface of the liquid should barely be seen to move.

During this long cooking time it is best to stir the contents occasionally and to check evaporation. When cooking on top of the fire rather than in the oven there is a chance that the food may burn if it is not stirred. Should the liquid have reduced, it should be replenished with water or stock. The amount of liquid in the finished dish is important since the correct concentration of seasonings will determine the richness and flavour. The liquid should not cover the meat being cooked as in boiling, but come part of the way up the sides.

An alternative to cooking the casserole on top of the fire is to turn the entire contents of the pan into a casserole and cook in the bottom two-thirds of the oven at a temperature not exceeding regulo 3, 170 °C (325 °F) for at least 2 hours. It can be cooked in a slower oven for a longer time, however, which is better still. A casserole cooked in an Aga overnight is perfect.

When the meat is cooked, the casserole is ready for thickening. There are several ways of doing this. In the recipe it is done with a flour-and-water paste. Blend the flour and water smoothly together in a cup to a lump-free 'cream', then blend some of the hot casserole liquid into this cream, whisking as you do so to prevent lumps forming. All this is then whisked back into the casserole and heated. As it comes to the boil it will thicken. Taste it, then *correct the seasoning*. This means that you should add sufficient extra salt and pepper, if necessary, to suit your taste. It is important to do this for every dish before serving.

It is possible that, although a recipe has been followed, the liquid is still too thin or perhaps too thick. If the liquid is thin, either continue to simmer it without the lid, to encourage evaporation, and it will then reduce; or make up a little more flour and water paste and proceed as before, starting with a teaspoon of flour blended with a little water.

To understand the use of alternative thickening agents and methods described in this book see the individual recipes that follow: goulash, in which potatoes are used, *boeuf bourguignonne* for the *roux* method, Lancashire hot pot in which the meat is simply dusted with flour, *coq au vin* which uses *beurre manié*, and white rabbit and pork casserole which uses cornflour. Usually these methods can be interchanged. As cooks develop their own preference for the different effects that the methods produce, so they will substitute one for another. Some prefer the clear glazed finish of a cornflour-thickened sauce, while others prefer to use flour. This comes with practice, and with experience you will 'casserole' without the recipe book, and make up your own ideas. It is a useful way of using up tired salad vegetables such as tomatoes, peppers and celery that may be wilting at the bottom of the refrigerator, and, if made in large quantities, any casserole will keep to reheat for more than one meal. The presence of wine or other acids (tomatoes, lemon) will improve the storage time of the dish since these slow down the growth of bacteria. A casserole will normally keep for a week in the refrigerator. For more than one meal, however, only reheat one serving at a time. When inventing your own recipes keep one dominant flavour only or use what is a good combination of two strong flavours: pork with orange and sweet peppers is an attractive blend as is lamb with mint, and they suit most tastes.

Beans, peas and lentils presoaked in clean cold water are an especially good addition to gammon, bacon and ham casseroles since they absorb the strong, salty, smoky flavours of these meats well. They also help to make a dish more substantial, and the amount of meat can be reduced if economy is a strong point. Normally the amount of meat to use per person is about 185 g when trimmed of gristle. In a dish with lots of extra vegetables and pulses (peas, beans, lentils), however, 450 g of meat would do for four persons.

It is a good idea to have several shapes and sizes of casseroles. A deep pot with a large belly and a narrower neck provides good all-round cooking and minimises evaporation.

A shallower dish can be used both for a casserole and as a gratin dish and is thus dual purpose. Most casseroles are meant to be taken straight from the oven to the table so must be attractive. A good range of country-style French cooking pots is available in London from Elizabeth David at 46 Bourne Street near Sloane Square and from David Mellor in Sloane Square itself.

COQ AU VIN

Chicken in red wine with bacon, mushrooms, garlic and shallots.

Recipes for this dish are numerous, the differences being not in the ingredients so much as in the methods used. The bird for *coq au vin* should be a free-range cockerel. It will have plenty of flavour but will be tough and need prolonged cooking to make it tender. But a tender roasting bird is often used since it is readily available and takes less time to cook. A Burgundian dish, *coq au vin* uses red wine as the cooking liquor or mostly wine with a little stock added. It can be red or white but it is more usual to use red. Bacon is included for flavour, either green (unsmoked) or smoked, and can be rashers or strips cut from a piece. The garnish, glazed shallots and button mushrooms, is the same as for another popular dish, *boeuf bourguignonne.* In fact, apart from the difference in the meats these two dishes are identical. *Coq au vin* can be further garnished with *croûtons* (triangles or other shapes of bread fried in butter until crisp and golden). If the dish needs prolonged cooking, the shallots and mushrooms should be added towards the end of cooking time so that they retain their character. The chicken itself can be cooked whole, but more often it is cut into pieces first. These are browned, either in a heavy-bottomed pan, or, more efficiently, by placing the pieces side by side in a roasting tin, brushing with butter and placing at the top of a very hot oven until they are the desired shade of brown. The residual fat is then poured away and the chicken flamed with brandy. If this step is omitted, care must be taken not to introduce more fat than is needed into the dish during its preparation.

Flambéeing a dish with brandy is done to burn off excessive fat. When the chicken has cooked, the liquor may have reduced itself during oven time into a thick sauce and need no additional starch liaison. In the following recipe, however, *beurre manié* (a paste of butter and flour) does the job and is added at the end. In some older recipes, the blood and the pounded liver are used to thicken the sauce, but this is not usual today. If this were done, however, care would be needed not to boil the sauce after the blood was added, otherwise it would *curdle* (separate out in lumps owing to coagulation of the protein). It should be noticed that the wine itself changes during cooking and becomes mellow. Initially it tastes raw, thus the wine also has to be cooked to give a good flavour. This rule applies to any dish in which wine or cider or beer is used as the main sauce ingredient.

With the chicken cooked, the wine sauce thickened and the seasoning corrected it is now ready for serving. This can be done from the casserole or, for more formal occasions, the chicken can be turned on to a heated dish and garnished with chopped parsley, bacon rolls and *croûtons.* For vegetables new boiled potatoes are best and if you want a green vegetable peas are an ideal accompaniment. If the chicken for this dish has been cooked whole it should be carved in the kitchen, arranged on a heated plate with the other ingredients over and around it, and garnished. Some cooks may have included the giblets during cooking for extra flavour (instead of using stock) and these should be removed before serving, together with the *bouquet garni* and the bayleaf.

4 to 6 pieces chicken; butter; 225 g button mushrooms; 225 g shallots or pickling onions; oil; 6 rashers streaky bacon; 1 clove garlic; 1 bottle red Burgundy; glass brandy (optional); 100 ml rich stock (optional); bayleaf; 1 tablespoon tomato purée; bouquet garni; salt and pepper; For beurre manié: 25 g butter; 25 g flour; For garnish: croûtons; bacon rolls; chopped parsley.

Preheat the oven to regulo 8, 230 °C (450 °F). Place the chicken pieces side by side in a roasting tin, brush lightly with melted butter and brown at the top of the oven; this takes about 10 minutes. Meanwhile wipe clean and trim the mushrooms and peel the shallots, leaving both whole. In a pan big enough to take the mushrooms in one layer heat a mixture of butter and oil — about 15 g of each — and sauté them in very hot fat, shaking the pan to brown them evenly on all sides; this takes about 1 minute. Remove from the pan and set aside. In the remaining fat repeat this process with the shallots, adding more fat if required (there should just be enough to cover the bottom of the pan in a thin film). Remove and set aside with the mushrooms. Remove the rind from the bacon, and chop.

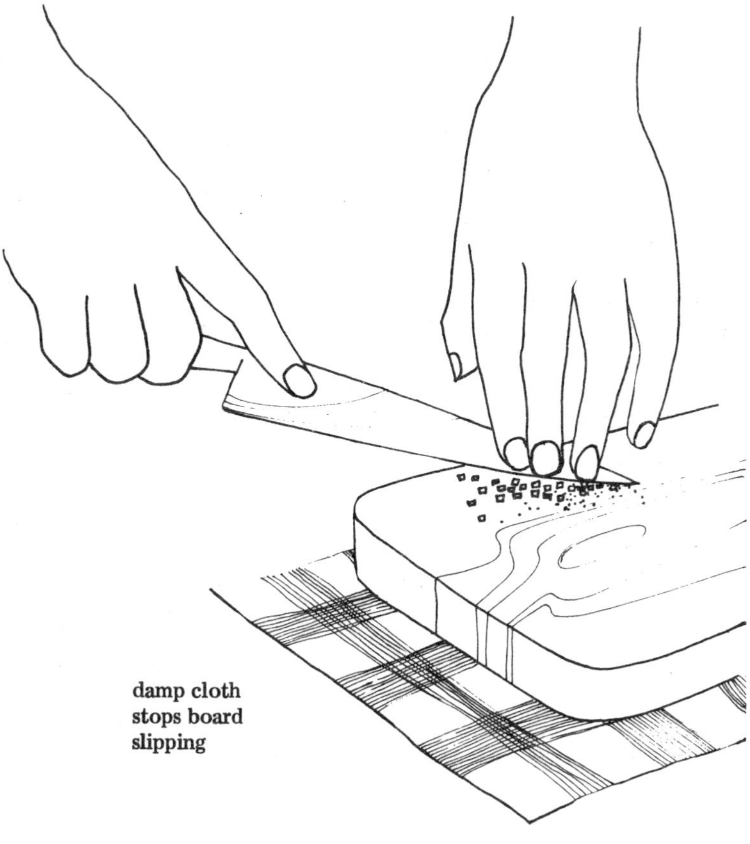

Figure 7.1 How to crush garlic

Remove the papery skin of the clove of garlic, then chop roughly (figure 7.1). Sprinkle the garlic with salt, then use pressure on the side of the knife to work it to a paste. The salt acts as an abrasive. A garlic-press is not necessary. When using a chopping board, stand it on a wrung-out cloth, which will stop the board sliding around the table and also stop it rattling should the table or the board be slightly uneven. Fry the mashed garlic in the same pan with the bacon, taking care that the garlic does not burn. Add the wine to the bacon and deglaze the pan, that is, you bring the wine to the boil, at the same time scraping the bits that have stuck to the bottom of the pan with a wooden spoon. The wine leaves the bottom of the saucepan clean. Set aside. Remove the chicken pieces from the oven and drain away the fat. Pour the brandy, if used, over the chicken and either ignite it with a match, or, if a gas cooker is used, carefully tip the roasting tin to one side so that the brandy is ignited at the edge by the flame. When the flames subside, place the chicken pieces in a casserole together with the wine and bacon, the stock if used, bayleaf, tomato purée, *bouquet garni* and salt and pepper, bearing in mind when seasoning that the bacon is salt and the garlic was crushed with salt earlier. Cover tightly and place in the bottom two-thirds of the oven, now lowered to regulo 3, 170 °C (325 °F) for 2 to 3 hours, the time depending on the quality of chicken used. Meanwhile, make the *beurre manié* by beating the butter with the flour to a paste. About 15 minutes before the end of cooking time, remove the casserole from the oven and stir in the *beurre manié*, a piece at a time until it has dispersed; this will thicken the sauce as it heats through. Add the shallots and mushrooms also to heat through. Correct the seasoning and either serve from the casserole or turn the entire contents on to a heated plate, sprinkle with parsley and tuck the *croûtons* around the edge. Grilled bacon rolls can also be included in the garnish. [*Serves 4 to 6*]

CROÛTONS

With a cutter stamp out shapes from stale thin slices of white bread. Fry on both sides in ½ cm of butter over a moderate heat until crisp and golden brown. Drain on kitchen paper.

WHITE RABBIT AND PORK CASSEROLE

A north-country dish.

> *2 legs of English tame white rabbit; 350 g lean belly pork on the bone; 2 large onions; 275 ml chicken stock; 2 heaped teaspoons dried sage; salt and pepper; To thicken: 2 level tablespoons cornflour blended to a cream with 3 tablepoons cold water.*

Put the rabbit into a casserole. Remove the bones from the piece of pork and reserve. Cut the pork into strips 2 cm wide. This makes it easier to remove the skin, which you then do by holding the strips skin side down and using a very sharp knife; skin it as if skinning fish. (Pork skin is very tough.)

Cut the meat into neat even-sized cubes 2 cm square, trimming off any large lumps of fat as or if necessary. Add the pork to the rabbit. Chop the onions very finely. They must be finely chopped to give the finished sauce the right kind of consistency and also to help thicken it; sliced onion does not have this effect.

Cut the onion in half, *leaving a piece of root on each half*; this is most important since it serves to hold the onion together. Remove the skin and cut off the shoot. Place the onion cut surface down on a chopping board and make three or four horizontal cuts towards *but not right through* the root end (figure 7.2*a*). Now, holding the point of the knife towards the root end, make five or six cuts vertically, again not allowing the point of the knife to protrude through the root end (figure 7.2*b*). Turn the knife round and cut crosswise as shown in figure 7.2*c*. You now have evenly chopped pieces of onion. If the onion is required finer, proceed to chop as shown on p. 78. To do this the point of the knife should be held down to the board with the left hand, while the right hand holding the knife chops up and down until the onion becomes as fine as you want it.

Add the onions to the meats in the saucepan together with the stock, sage, salt and pepper. Separate the pork bones and bury them underneath the other ingredients in the saucepan. The reason for doing this is to provide the finished dish with more flavour extracted from the bones during cooking. It is a neat, efficient way of using the bones to introduce flavour

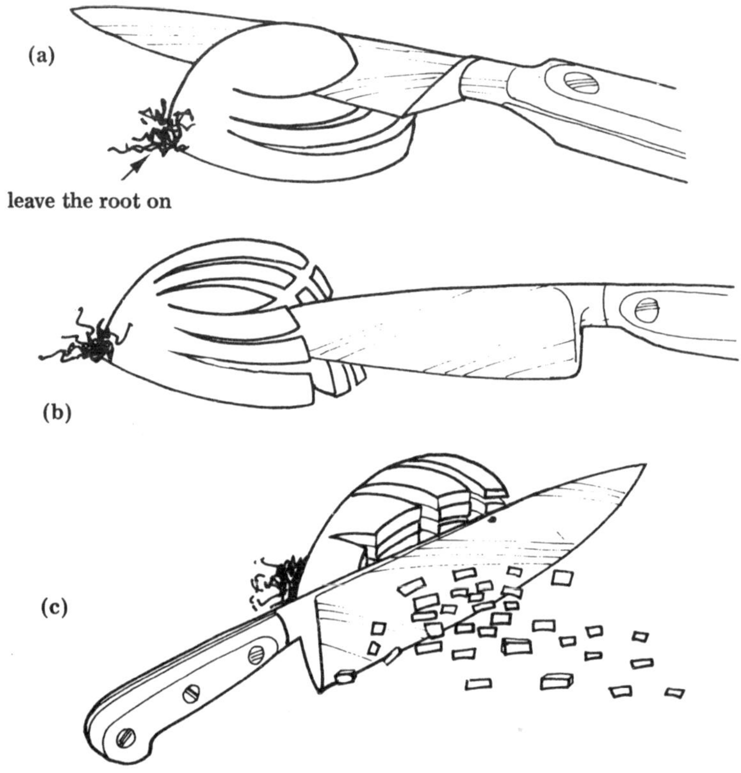

Figure 7.2 How to chop an onion

and in a homely dish such as this the fact that it is an unsophisticated method is not relevant. Bring the saucepan ingredients to the boil, then turn down to the barest simmer, and cover with a tight-fitting lid. Cook in this way for 1½ hours or until the meat is cooked. You can stir the ingredients every half hour or so. A stew or casserole cooked on top of the fire stands more chance of sticking to the bottom of the pan than if cooked in the oven. When the meat is done, trickle in the stirred cornflour-and-water mixture, stirring as you do so. Allow the sauce to come to the boil, when it will thicken. Remove the bones. Correct the seasoning. Serve with boiled or mashed potatoes and a green vegetable.

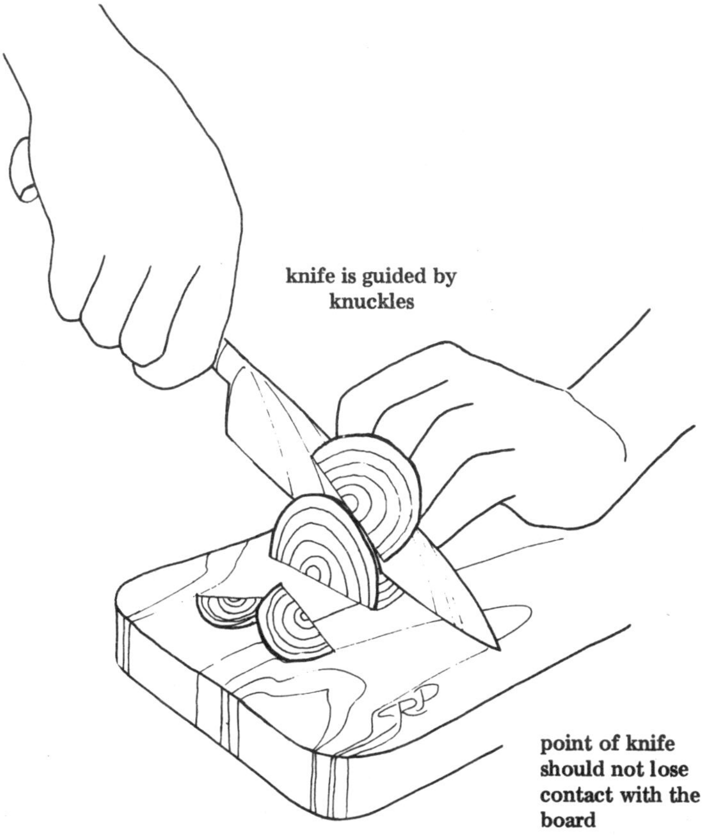
knife is guided by knuckles
point of knife should not lose contact with the board

Figure 7.3 How to slice an onion

The following instructions are for slicing onions (chopping, not slicing, was required for the dish above). Cut the onion in half, *leaving a piece of root on each half.* This is most important since it holds the onion together while you slice it. Cut off the shoot and remove the skin. Place the onion cut side down on the board. Steady it using the fingertips so that the knife is guided by the knuckles which should be in an upright position. Slice downwards, pushing the knife *away* from you as you do so. The point of the knife should never leave the board but slide backwards and forwards with each slicing (figure 7.3).

Figure 7.4 How to chop vegetables finely

To chop vegetables finely the point of the knife should be held down on the board with the left hand while the right hand holds the handle and chops up and down (figure 7.4). The point of the knife should never lose contact with the board; in this way you have more control of the knife and it is therefore less tiring. If the board is unsteady stand it on a wrung-out cloth.

CARBONNADE FLAMANDE

Beef stewed in beer.

1 kg stewing steak; 2 large onions; 25 g butter; 2 tablespoons oil; 1 clove garlic; salt and pepper; 575 ml beer; bayleaf; bouquet garni; 1 dessertspoon vinegar; 2 to 3 teaspoons sugar; 1 tablespoon flour; 3 tablespoons water.

Cut the meat into strips of about 1 cm by 7 cm long, discarding any gristle. Slice the onions. In a large saucepan, heat the butter and oil together and in it sauté the meat a few pieces at a time over a brisk heat until a dark rich brown.

Remove the pieces to a plate as you do so. Add the onions and continue to cook over a moderate heat until they are soft; this takes about 7 minutes. Mash the garlic with salt and add to the pan with the onions. Return all the meat to the pan together with the salt and pepper, beer, bayleaf, *bouquet garni*, vinegar and sugar. Bring to just under the boil, scraping the bits from the bottom of the pan as you do so, that is, deglaze the pan. To cook, either cover the pan tightly and continue on the lowest heat possible over the fire for about 2 hours, or turn the entire contents of the pan into a casserole and cook, covered, in the bottom two-thirds of the oven at regulo 3, 170 °C (325 °F) for 2 hours or until the meat is tender. The time may be longer and depends on the quality of the meat.

Meanwhile, mix the flour to a smooth cream with the water and add to the casserole about 15 minutes before the dish is finally taken from the oven; stir in well. To prevent lumps forming it is best to whisk a little of the hot liquid into the flour-and-water and then whisk it all back in the casserole. Correct the seasoning. Serve with boiled potatoes. (The method is described in more detail at the beginning of this chapter.) [*Serves 4 to 6*]

The flour and water mixture will lower the temperature of the stew, so it is important that it be allowed to come back to temperature. Also, the flour is uncooked when it is added so it must be allowed to heat through properly, when the starch grains in the flour will swell and burst, thus causing the thin liquid to thicken into a sauce.

GULYAS

Goulash — an Hungarian stew of meat and vegetables, red and spicy, with paprika pepper, and thickened with potatoes.

Like most casseroles this Hungarian variation is a wholesome and unsophisticated dish which should have lots of potatoes and paprika pepper. A popular variation is to add soured cream, stirred in just before serving. The traditional accompaniment is buttered noodles sprinkled with caraway seeds. There are many versions of goulash, however, even a meatless goulash soup! The meaning is 'stewed', and goulash should be considered a generic name for a variety of dishes made with pork, beef, veal, lamb, game or a combination of meats. Seasonings additional to paprika include caraway seeds, marjoram and garlic. Crush the seeds on a board using the back of a teaspoon: this bruises them to release more flavour. (This applies to any seeds used in cooking if they are to be added whole rather than powdered.) The cooking liquor is usually water, although a dry white wine can be used instead. Another variation is to stir in large quantities of cooked sauerkraut just before serving, making a Transylvanian (*skekely*) goulash. In any event, goulash must have plenty of onions in it.

> *350 g veal; 350 g beef; 500 g onions; 1 clove garlic; 50 g fat; 2 tablespoons paprika pepper; 275 ml tomato pulp; salt and pepper; water; 1 teaspoon caraway seeds; ½ teaspoon marjoram; 450 g potatoes; 150 ml soured cream.*

Cut the meat into pieces, slice the onions and mash the garlic with salt. Heat the fat in a saucepan and in it lightly brown the meat a few pieces at a time, removing them to a plate as you do so. In the fat that remains, soften the onions over a moderate heat until golden brown, together with the garlic; this takes about 10 minutes. Add more fat if required. Return the pieces of meat to the pan and add the paprika, tomato pulp, salt and pepper, and barely cover with water. Bring to just under the boil. Add the caraway seeds and marjoram, cover and cook over a very low heat for 2 hours or until the meat is done. Alternatively, the contents of the pan can be turned into a casserole and placed in the bottom two-thirds of the oven set at regulo 3, 170 °C (325 °F). Meanwhile, peel and slice the potatoes (keep them under cold water to prevent discolouring). After about 1 hour add the potatoes to the meat and mix well in. The potatoes and paprika both swell during cooking, forming a thick sauce. No additional thickening should therefore be necessary. The potatoes may take longer to cook through than you think, taking about three times as long as when cooked on their own in boiling water. Serve from the casserole with the soured cream stirred in just at the last minute. Alternatively, turn into a heated dish. Serve with buttered noodles.

[*Serves 4*]

BOEUF A LA BOURGUIGNONNE

Beef cooked in red wine with bacon, mushrooms, shallots and garlic.

A well-known dish from Burgundy, *boeuf à la bourguignonne* is the sister dish to *coq au vin*, the only difference being the meats used. The cubes of meat for this dish should be browned in fat until almost black, giving a very dark sauce. Because browning the meat in this way tends to toughen the meat slightly it is best to use a better-quality beef, rump or topside in preference to stewing beef. This dish is served with new boiled potatoes, but often plain boiled rice or noodles are served instead. There are many methods of making this classic dish. Here is one of them.

> *125 g streaky bacon rashers or a piece; oil; 225 g button mushrooms; 225 g shallots or pickling onions; 750 g topside of beef or other braising steak; 1 clove garlic; 25 g flour; 575 ml red wine; 300 ml beef stock; bouquet garni; bayleaf; salt and pepper.*

Preheat the oven to regulo 3, 170 °C (325 °F). Chop the bacon or dice the piece into 1 cm cubes. Heat one tablespoon of oil in a saucepan and in it sauté the bacon. As the pieces brown, transfer them to a casserole. Meanwhile, wipe and trim the mushrooms and peel the onions, leaving both whole. In the fat that remains, sauté the mushrooms quickly, shaking the pan from side to side to brown on all sides. Do this over a brisk heat. Remove the mushrooms to a plate and set aside. Adding more oil if necessary to what remains in the pan, sauté the onions, shaking the pan from side to side so that they brown evenly on all sides. Put with the mushrooms. Cut the meat into even-sized pieces and, in the same pan, sauté a few at a time, adding more oil if necessary. There should be enough oil to cover the base of the pan with a thin film. Use a wooden long-handled spoon to turn the meat and as it turns a dark brown lift into the casserole with the bacon. On no account put all the meat at once into the pan, otherwise the temperature of the oil will be reduced so much that it will not seal the meat and it will begin to stew in its own juice. Mash the garlic with salt and add to the bacon. After all the meat has been browned and removed from the pan there should be about 2 tablespoons of dripping remaining. Add the flour to this and cook for a few minutes over a moderate heat, stirring constantly. The flour should be allowed to brown. You now have a brown *roux*. A little at a time, and stirring constantly between each addition and the next, add the wine until it is all used up, scraping the meaty bits sticking to the bottom and sides of the pan as you do so. Bring to the boil. The wine has the effect of cleaning the pan — it is deglazing. Add the stock. You should now have a thickened but still raw wine sauce. Pour this over the meat in the casserole, bury the *bouquet garni* and bayleaf underneath, season with salt and pepper and cook in the bottom two-thirds of the oven for 2 hours or until the meat is tender. Fifteen to twenty minutes before the casserole is ready, add the mushrooms and shallots to heat through. Finally correct the seasoning and serve the *boeuf bourguignonne* from the casserole. [*Serves 4*]

LANCASHIRE HOT POT

A simple stew of lamb, potatoes and onions cooked in water or stock, sometimes with pearl barley added.

> *6 large potatoes; 4 large onions; 750 g neck of lamb chops; 2 lambs' kidneys (optional); 25 g flour; salt and pepper; 50 g pearl barley; 200 ml boiling stock or water; butter.*

Preheat the oven to regulo 3, 170 °C (325 °F). Peel the potatoes and cut into slices, keeping under cold water to prevent browning. Slice the onion thinly. Trim the lamb of unwanted fat or gristle. Remove the core from the kidneys, if used, and discard. Slice the kidneys. Dust the kidneys and meat with seasoned flour. In a large casserole, layer these ingredients together, seasoning as you go, scattering in the pearl barley. End with a layer of potatoes. Pour the stock over. Brush the top with butter. Cover the casserole with the lid and place in the bottom two-thirds of the oven. Cook for 2 hours. Remove the lid and return to the oven, turned up to regulo 6, 200 °C (400 °F) to brown the top. Serve from the casserole.

8

Fluffy Rice

You must accept from the start that to produce perfectly cooked rice the cooking time must be precise and match the type of grain used. There are many thousands of types of rice grain. It is therefore not really possible for any cookery book to give precise instructions on how to cook rice — it can only act as a guide.

You may have assumed that there are only a handful of varieties of rice, including a short stubby grain (suitable for making milk puddings because it cooks soft and sticky), a medium grain often referred to as Carolina rice and a long grain called Patna rice. It was from Carolina in the United States and from Patna in Bengal that the majority of rice used to come and these names have persisted. In addition you may know of Basmati rice, also from India, Arborio rice from Italy and Spanish Valencia rice. These, however, are only a few of over seven thousand varieties, not to mention the specially treated grains known as parboiled, pre-fluffed and pre-cooked. (When a rice has been treated by one of these methods it cannot be cooked as normal. You must follow the directions on the manufacturer's label.) There is also a more natural, unpolished rice usually referred to as brown rice. Because it is only slightly milled it retains the valuable vitamins and minerals present in the bran — the brownish outer skin that lies beneath the husk. It has a chewy texture and nutty taste. Brown rice is available from health food shops. It takes a comparatively long time to cook.

In the original rice-producing countries of the east where

it forms an important staple food, rice is sold in shops or from stalls specialising in nothing else. Sacks of it are arranged across the floor, containing many varieties and qualities of unsorted, unwashed grain. A customer will lift a handful to his nose and an expert will be able to tell from the smell how good the sample is. Poor rice, in addition to not having a certain aroma, contains foreign matter and has many broken grains. Much of the best rice is exported, leaving the rice-producers themselves with less choice than we have in England. We are offered a wide variety of good quality rice that has been sorted, graded and washed and is ready to use straight from the packet. Most of the rice grown for export today comes from the United States and conforms to very high standards of cleanliness. When choosing rice it is worth paying extra for good quality that has a brand name. Although one packet of rice may look much the same as any other, assume that it is not. The difference will become apparent as you cook it. Some of the cheaper long-grain rice goes to pudding as it cooks, whereas the more expensive better quality rice cooks evenly and keeps separate.

It is not for every occasion that separate grains are desirable, however — imagine using chopsticks for this and how impossible it would be to eat. In Chinese and Japanese cooking rice must be cooked to become sticky and thus can be manipulated with chopsticks.

When cooking rice it is possible to achieve the same result by one of several methods. The advocates of each method will argue that theirs is the one and only method. This is probably because they use the same kind of rice each time and cook it in exactly the same way. If, on the other hand, they were to switch to a different brand the result would not necessarily be the same. Basically, rice is cooked either in a large amount of boiling salted water, or a very precise amount of water is used which is absorbed into the rice at exactly the same rate as it takes to cook. This second principle can be carried out in a saucepan on top of the fire or it can be done in the oven. Try both methods and continue with whichever suits you and the purpose for which it is being used.

TO COOK RICE

Absorption method. A quick and easy way especially suited to good quality washed rice.

> *1 teacupful good quality long-grain rice (175 g); 2 teacupfuls water; 1 level teaspoon salt.*

You need a saucepan with a tight-fitting lid. Put the rice, water and salt into the pan (always double the amount of water to rice) and bring to the boil. Immediately lower the heat to as low as it will go and place the lid on the pan tightly. Allow to cook gently for 15 minutes. Remove from the heat and allow to stand undisturbed for a further 5 minutes. The rice will continue to cook in the residual heat. Do not stir the rice at any time during this 20 minutes, otherwise the grains become sticky; in fact, do not even lift the lid of the pan to have a look, otherwise steam will escape, and it is the steam that helps it to cook. After 20 minutes all the water will have been absorbed. Test a grain to check that it is cooked through, then use a fork quickly and lightly to fluff the rice up. Never pat cooked rice down to make it flat. Once cooked it is a very delicate thing so treat it very gently.

Note These instructions can be modified slightly according to the kind of long-grain rice you are using. Bear in mind that the cooking time is between 12 and 20 minutes. Cooked rice will lump together if allowed to stand for more than 10 minutes in the pan in which it was cooked. It should be fluffed up fairly soon and either served or used for whichever purpose it was meant. If it is meant for a salad, you should toss in the vinaigrette dressing and other items while it is still fresh and hot.

The absorption method of cooking rice can be carried out in the oven. Use exactly the same amount of rice, water and salt as in the recipe above but boil the water first. Put into a casserole, cover tightly and cook for 40 minutes on the middle shelf of the oven set at regulo 4, 180 °C (350 °F). *Jambalaya*, a rice dish from the Mississippi, is cooked according to the same principle. The addition of onions, garlic, gammon, tomatoes and spices makes no real difference to the method of cooking (see p. 87).

The amount of rice to allow is 60 g per person. One ordinary teacupful holds 175 g, enough for three people. These are modest amounts, however, and would not satisfy an eastern appetite. For large helpings allow up to 125 g per person. Remember that there is no need to wash pre-packed washed rice again. All American rice that is exported has been washed and is ready for use. If on the other hand you are using rice delivered to this country in burlap (sacks) from India, Italy or Spain, it is essential to wash and sort it before cooking. This type of rice is known as commodity rice and contains grit and other foreign matter that should be removed as you wash it. When you have washed the rice, do not be tempted to leave it soaking or allow it to stand with water clinging to it. In this way the grain swells and it cannot then be cooked in the normal way. Use it immediately.

If you have a quantity of rice that tends to become sticky during cooking, on a subsequent occasion you can improve matters by frying the rice initially in a small amount of fat. Use about 15 g butter or other fat to one teacupful of rice. Put the butter and rice into the saucepan and fry for a few minutes, shaking the pan occasionally or stirring with a wooden spoon. It does not matter if the grains become slightly browned at this stage. This method hardens the outside of the grain somewhat and they remain separate during cooking. When you have fried the rice, proceed as usual. (This method of frying the rice bears no resemblance to Chinese fried rice.)

TO COOK RICE

Boiling water method.

> *1½ l water; 1 rounded teaspoon salt; 1 teacupful good-quality long-grain rice (175 g).*

When cooking more rice, increase the amount of water accordingly. It does not matter if there is more water than required, however. In a large pan, bring the water and salt to the boil. Add the rice in a thin stream and cook without the lid for 12 to 15 minutes or until a grain is cooked when tested between the finger and thumb. Drain the rice into a colander or sieve. You can run fresh hot water through it to remove any remaining traces of starch but this should not be necessary. Cover the colander with a dry cloth and allow to stand for 5 minutes. The rice will continue to dry out while the cloth absorbs the steam as it rises. Some people prefer to dry out the rice by spreading it on a tray and standing it in a warm oven (turned off) for a few minutes.

Once cooked, rice keeps well in the refrigerator for up to 7 days. Day-old rice makes excellent Chinese fried rice (see p. 88). Otherwise, to reheat rice in the normal way, put into a saucepan with a few tablespoons of water, put on the lid and shake the pan occasionally as it warms through over a gentle heat. Fork up and serve.

Pre-cooked rice is rice that has been fully cooked after milling, then dried. It only needs reconstituting in much the same way as dried vegetables or soup, and should be done according to the instructions on the packet. Special steam treatment before milling results in par-boiled and pre-fluffed rice. This drives many of the vitamins and minerals into the grain itself; these are therefore not lost during subsequent milling as they normally would be. To cook follow the instructions on the packet.

JAMBALAYA

A Creole dish of baked rice, gammon, peppers and onions. Mississippi River *jambalaya* includes prawns as well. The amounts of everything are really up to the cook or according to the likes of the family. It works on the principle that rice will absorb about twice its own volume of liquid in cooking; bear in mind that juicy tomatoes can be counted as liquid too. The following recipe works well but you can change it about.

> *1 onion; 3 to 4 tablespoons oil or dripping; 2 cloves garlic; 1 green or red pepper; 150 g raw gammon, weighed after trimming; 175 g long-grain rice; 3 canned or fresh tomatoes made up to ½ l with stock, cider or water; a few drops Tabasco; a pinch marjoram and thyme.*

Preheat the oven to regulo 6, 200 °C (400 °F). Chop the onion. Heat the oil or dripping and start to soften the onion while you mash the garlic with salt and chop the pepper. Add the garlic and pepper. Cut the gammon into 7 mm dice, bearing in mind that it has to cook in the same time as the rice; make all the cubes the same size so that they cook evenly. Add the gammon and the rice to the pan and cook for a few minutes, stirring as you do so. Add all the other ingredients, bring to the boil, then turn the entire contents into a large casserole. Cover with a tight-fitting lid then place in the middle of the oven to cook for a further 35-40 minutes, or until the rice is done and has absorbed all the liquid. It is a good idea to stir the contents of the casserole about half way through cooking to make sure that no rice grains are becoming hard round the edges. Serve from the casserole or turn the entire contents on to a heated dish. [*Serves 3 to 4*]

CHINESE FRIED RICE

Plain boiled white rice tossed up with egg, onion, bacon, peas or whatever else you may have that is suitable. It is adaptable. A good way of making use of yesterday's rice.

> *1 teacupful long-grain rice (175 g); 1 to 2 eggs; 1 small onion; 2 rashers streaky bacon; 50 g frozen peas; half a red pepper; 50 g lard; salt and pepper.*

Cook the rice according to the directions on p. 85. Beat the eggs with a fork until the yolks and whites are mixed. Chop the onion and the bacon rashers very finely. Defrost the peas. Cut the pepper into dice. In a large saucepan melt half the quantity of lard and gently sauté the onion and bacon until soft but not browned. Toss in the hot boiled rice and mix gently, using if possible a long-handled metal spoon. (If you use a thick wooden spoon it will mash the rice grains.) Gently push the rice mixture to one side of the pan, leaving the other clear. Melt the remaining lard, tilting the pan to one side as you do so to prevent it running underneath the rice on the other side. Pour in the egg and gently scramble it. Take care not to allow any raw egg to mix in with the rice at this stage. When the egg is completely coagulated gently toss it together with the rice. Add the peas and pepper. Season with salt and pepper. Put the lid on the pan and allow the peas and pepper to heat through for a minute over a low heat. Turn the entire contents of the pan on to a heated dish and serve.

Note If using up left-over boiled rice that has gone cold, reheat it first by putting a few tablespoons of water in a saucepan, adding the rice and heating gently with the lid on.

You can incorporate other ingredients into this dish such as mushrooms, sweetcorn, spring onions and chopped bits of meat. Made substantially it can become a lunch or supper dish by itself. Chinese fried rice should be sticky so that it can be eaten with chopsticks. [*Serves 3*]

CHICKEN AND RICE SALAD

The rice used for this and any other cold dish should be mixed with the dressing and seasonings while the rice is still hot — in this way it absorbs them.

1 teacupful long-grain rice; Vinaigrette: 3 tablespoons oil; 1 tablespoon wine vinegar; ½ teaspoon dry mustard; salt and pepper. 50 g sultanas; 1 level teaspoon curry powder; 50 g chopped walnuts or toasted flaked almonds; 2 sticks celery; 1 cupful cooked chicken.

Cook the rice according to the instructions on p. 86. Make the vinaigrette by combining the oil, vinegar, mustard plus salt and pepper to taste in a screw-top jar. Shake well to mix. Carefully toss the hot cooked rice and the vinaigrette together in a large bowl. Add the sultanas, curry powder and nuts. Chop the celery and the chicken and add these. Correct the seasoning. Heap on to a large serving platter.

[*Serves 3 to 4*]

BROWN RICE

Bhuna chaval — Indian. Treated in the following way rice grains stay separated, including poor quality rice that would otherwise go to pudding.

> *25 g butter or other clean fat; 1 heaped tablespoon finely chopped onion; 1 teacupful (175 g) long-grain rice; 2 teacupfuls water; 1 level teaspoon salt.*

Melt the butter in a saucepan with a tight-fitting lid. Add the onion and rice, and fry until both are brown, stirring constantly. Add 2 teacupfuls water and the salt (there will be a lot of hissing). Bring to the boil, then fit the lid on tightly, lower the heat to as low as it will go and allow to cook for 20 minutes. (Do not lift the lid and allow the steam to escape during this time, and do not stir the rice.) Now the water will all have been absorbed by the rice and the rice will be cooked. Brown rice can be served as a change from white rice. [*Serves 3*]

RISOTTO MILANESE

Italian. This classic method of preparing rice to be eaten as a dish in its own right is simply rice flavoured with butter, saffron, parmesan cheese, chicken stock and onion. Some recipes also contain bone-marrow. Most people, however, are more familiar with risottos brightly coloured with vegetables and cooked meats. This one remains a golden saffron yellow.

> *1 small onion; 25 g butter; 1 teacupful (175 g) Arborio or long-grain rice; a pinch saffron; water; 725 ml light chicken stock; To serve: 25 g butter; 25 g Parmesan cheese.*

Chop the onion very finely. Slowly melt the butter in a large pan and in it soften the onion. Neither the butter nor the onion must be allowed to brown, the onions should almost melt. Stir in the rice and coat with the fat. Meanwhile, put the saffron into a small saucepan and heat gently over a low heat until it becomes crisp. Crumble the saffron when cool enough to handle to a powder between the finger and thumb. Add half a cup of water to the saffron, bring just to the boil, then set aside and allow to infuse while the risotto is being made. Have the chicken stock simmering in a separate pan. To make the risotto, which takes about 20 minutes, the cook should stir and attend to it constantly. Proceed by adding a small amount of the stock to the rice and stir until it has all been absorbed, after which you then add some more and continue in the same way. The pan is left uncovered the whole time. When the rice is almost cooked add the saffron. Risotto milanese should be glossy. Stir in the additional butter and grated Parmesan cheese and season to taste. You can serve with even more butter and Parmesan cheese separately on the table. [*Serves 3*]

Note A great deal of evaporation takes place while the rice cooks, which is why a larger amount of liquid is required than for cooking rice by the absorption method described on p. 85, where the lid is kept tightly on the pan all through. You may find that the rice is cooked without using the full amount of stock given in the recipe; the amount depends on how much evaporation takes place as a result of using a small or a large pan, and the quantity of rice in it. A large pan has a bigger surface area so more stock would be required.

9

Cooking Vegetables

Without both fruit and vegetables it would be very difficult to achieve a balanced meal or diet whether viewed from a nutritional or an aesthetic angle. Many people consider that the success of a meal stands or falls on the care and skill given to the preparation and service of vegetables. That the nutritional value of plant food is vital to our health is a well recognised fact, but some vegetables are so sensitive to the treatment given to them after harvesting — in storage and in cooking — that they are probably useless as food by the time they are consumed. So the important thing is not simply to have vegetables, but to have vegetables cooked and served in optimum condition. We should optimise their nutritional content together with colour, aroma, texture and flavour. Unfortunately there often has to be a compromise because no one cookery method suits all these factors.

Nutritionally vegetables provide vitamins, minerals and roughage. Roughage in the context of food is another name for the cellulose of plants which is eaten as a necessary aid to good digestion. Vitamin C found in fruit and vegetables is not present in other foods; great care must be taken to preserve it since it is easily destroyed by careless cooking, or if the vegetable that contains it has been allowed to wilt. Ideally, from the nutritional aspect alone, it is best to eat vegetables raw, soon after harvesting. From then on, vitamin C starts being destroyed by the action of enzymes that are also present in the vegetable. It is a fact that frozen vegetables, supplied by reputable frozen food manufacturers, contain more vitamin C (because they are harvested and frozen almost immediately) than most of the vegetables available in greengrocers. Peas, for example, are frozen within half-an-hour of being pulled at a freezing plant on site. Freezing does not destroy vitamin C, but it halts the action of bacteria and retards enzymatic growth.

The vegetables we eat come from all parts of the plant, according to the kind of vegetable. The parts are roots, bulbous roots, tubers, blanched stems, leaves, flowers and—it may not have occurred to you—fruits in the case of aubergines and tomatoes. They are variously suited to being cooked by boiling, steaming, baking, frying, deep-frying, grilling and braising. There is not the space to consider each vegetable cooked by each method. Instead, what follows are more general observations which should help you.

But before any cooking, good marketing is important. Top quality fruit and vegetables will be nourishing and appetising. Buy as much as you need for immediate consumption (with the exception of root vegetables, which store well). Best quality needs no description in most cases but speaks for itself: heavy fruit full of juice, onions so firm and dry that they rustle in the sack, bright green crispy leaves, a hard white head of cauliflower and so on. Some fruits are harvested under-ripe and may be bought as such—bananas and pears, for example—and these should be stored at room temperature to hasten enzymatic activity, which brings them to the peak of ripeness. Otherwise fruit and vegetables should be stored at temperatures just above freezing, between 2 and 4 °C, which delays enzymatic and chemical changes. Tropical fruits should be stored at room temperature, however. (You may have seen bananas that have accidentally been allowed to catch the frost around Christmas time and which usually have to be sold off cheaply because of their condition.) Temperature is not the only factor. To store fruit and vegetables, there must be the right amount of humidity, and they must be packed to allow air to circulate through. They continue to breathe after harvesting, and require both air and moisture; the salad tray at the bottom of a refrigerator with its cover has been specially designed to meet these conditions.

When we cook vegetables it is to soften or to gelatinise the cellulose in them. Moisture is needed for this which in some cases is provided by the vegetable itself, for example, tomatoes, or it has to be provided by steaming or boiling, for example, beans, carrots, asparagus, globe artichokes, etc. Those that already contain sufficient water can be cooked by one of the dry heat methods — baking, grilling or frying. Potatoes can be baked because they contain an adequate amount of water to gelatinise the starch present, but they can also be boiled or steamed. Obviously the more cellulose there is in a plant, the longer it takes to cook. One of the most versatile of vegetables is the potato which can be cooked by any of the cookery methods mentioned. Because potatoes absorb water in boiling, they are also capable of taking on other flavours which we might wish to introduce. For instance, we can boil them in chicken stock instead of in plain water, or we can roast them in meat drippings — any of these will be absorbed and thus add flavour. There are many varieties of potato, however, each one suited to a particular method of preparation. For sautéed potatoes, boiled potatoes and potato salad, a waxy variety should be chosen, while for mashing, for chips and for baking, a floury potato is best. Floury potatoes contain less water than waxy ones. As their name suggests they are mealy in texture and make excellent fluffy mash. However, for sautéed potatoes and boiled potatoes, which must be firm and retain their shape well during cooking, the waxy kind are best suited. Immature potatoes, whether waxy or floury, contain more water than full-grown potatoes and are therefore also well suited to boiling, sautéeing and making into salads.

Green vegetables (which, together with citrus fruits, we rely on for vitamin C) should be plunged into a saucepan containing sufficient boiling salted water to cover, and cooked without a lid until just tender. In addition to making the vegetables tender we must try (1) to avoid the destruction of vitamin C and (2) to preserve the bright green colour. It is easy to lose the vitamin: too much water will leach it out; heat and overcooking will also destroy it as will air dissolved in the cooking water, which is why the water is boiled first to remove air. So we must cook the vegetable as quickly as possible in a minimum of water. Enzymes that are present in the vegetable are also responsible for destroying vitamin C, and they are themselves destroyed by heat. (It is for this reason that vegetables are blanched quickly before being put in the deep-freeze.) We are told to cook green vegetables in an uncovered pan: this is to preserve the greenness of them. When vegetables boil in water they give off volatile acids which evaporate into steam. If there is a lid to the pan, these will condense back into the cooking water and cause the bright green chlorophyll to become an olive green colour instead. This pigment is unstable in acidic conditions, turning a dull green. It is not stable with heat either, so care must be taken to cook for the minimum amount of time. Now although an alkaline solution, achieved by adding soda to the water, will preserve the green colour, it will not only make the vegetable turn mushy and taste awful, but will also take its toll of vitamin C and thiamin. These are the explanations for cooking green vegetables in the manner stated above: for the preservation of nutrients and the preservation of colour. Remember that on no account should soda be added to the water in which green vegetables are to be cooked.

In addition to chlorophyll, other pigments are responsible for different colorations—flavones, carotenes, anthocyanins and lycopenes.

Flavones are the white pigments found in onions, potatoes and cauliflowers. A pinch of cream of tartar added to the cooking water of these vegetables helps preserve the whiteness of them. Unlike chlorophyll, which is unstable to heat, flavones are not affected and remain the same colour. However, and again unlike chlorophyll which is stable in an alkaline solution, flavones turn yellow in alkali. The water in which the vegetable is cooked also turns yellow, showing that flavones are water soluble. If your tap water is hard (alkaline) you can neutralise it with a pinch of cream of tartar and use it for keeping boiled onions, cauliflower and potato white.

So far we have seen that heat, acids and alkalis are likely to affect the colours of vegetables and that heat and alkalis destroy vitamin C and thiamin.

Most instructions for cooking red cabbage include a tart apple in the recipe. There are two red pigments in red vegetables and the one responsible for the red colour in red cabbage is anthocianin, which is also found in cherries, currants and beetroot. It becomes unstable in alkali, turning a bluish-purple colour, but with acid it remains unchanged. It is for this reason that some acid is included when cooking red cabbage. In this case the tart apple provides the acid. Red fruit, however, usually contains enough acid in itself to keep it stable. Anthocyanin is water soluble; it is not affected by heat. It reacts violently to certain other factors, turning blue-black on contact with tannin or with iron. Care has therefore to be taken when mixing up fruit punches in which tea is an ingredient because, once the colour has changed, nothing can be done to reverse the process.

The pigment responsible for the colour in red wines is another red pigment, called lycopene. It is closely related to carotene, which is yellow and found in carrots, peaches and apricots. Neither lycopene nor carotene is water soluble; both are stable to heat and to acids and alkalis. Lycopene, however, is soluble in alcohol, which accounts for the red colour in wines. Carotene is also found in green vegetables but the colour is masked by chlorophyll. It becomes apparent when a green vegetable has wilted badly, turning yellow.

Having considered the colours of vegetables we shall now look again into how nutrients can be preserved. When preparing vegetables with skins that have to be peeled, peel thinly. The nutrients in many cases lie just under the skin, which is a good reason for leaving the skin on if at all possible. Many root vegetables, for example, artichokes, carrots, potatoes, are quite acceptable cooked in their skins when well scrubbed and, in the case of potatoes, the skins can be removed after boiling. Dried lentils should be sorted, washed, soaked overnight and then cooked in their soaking liquid *without* salt, with the addition of a little soda. Legumes (peas, beans and lentils) and dried fruits should always be soaked for several hours or overnight before being cooked. This increases the volume of the finished product. They should then be cooked in their soaking liquid, and in this way the nutrients lost by leaching will be recaptured. Legumes are best cooked in slightly alkaline water, which will speed the cooking. Use $^1/_8$ teaspoon of soda to 3 l of non-alkaline (soft) tap water. Apart from dried legumes, no other vegetable should be prepared ahead of time, or left soaking in water. Potatoes, however, can be kept under cold water while they are being prepared. Some fruits and vegetables discolour when the raw surface is exposed to air, including potatoes, Jerusalem artichokes, apples, pears and bananas. This can be prevented in several ways: keeping under water is one of them. Other methods include brushing or dipping in an acid, usually lemon or pineapple, or brushing with ascorbic acid, or using a commercial antioxidant. The disadvantage of soaking any fruit or vegetable in water is that it leaches out vitamins and minerals. Fruits and vegetables are thus best prepared and cut up as they are required. Leaving cut surfaces exposed to the air for any length of time also results in spoilage through oxidation.

There are ways in which flavours can be preserved or modified if too strong. Flavours are highly volatile organic compounds (esters, ketones, aldehydes) which are lost by evaporation. Fats, however, absorb flavours so it is possible to capture the flavours in oil by frying them first, or by adding a little oil to the cooking liquid of boiled vegetables. Frying a vegetable not only captures the flavour but can also change it, as in the case of onions. Onions contain a large amount of sugar which changes to caramel when they are fried, becoming sweeter. Delicately flavoured vegetables should be cooked briefly in a small amount of water with the lid on (unless a green vegetable). Since flavours are water soluble, it is self-evident that vegetables should be cooked in this way in order to retain as much of the flavour as possible. Conversely, strongly flavoured vegetables should be cooked in a large pan with plenty of water and without a lid. The timing is important because some vegetables become stronger in flavour the longer they are cooked, for example, cauliflower, while some, like onions, become milder. If a delicate vegetable is suitable (that is, if it is not a vegetable that packs closely), steam it. There is less loss by leaching.

Cabbage and spinach are best boiled in a saucepan, while cauliflower and potatoes can be successfully steamed. There are two reasons why cabbage and spinach should not be steamed. One is that they are likely to lose their fresh green colour since the volatile acids are not able to evaporate, but condense back on to the vegetable, causing the chlorophyll to become an olive green colour. The other is that the nature of these two vegetables does not allow heat to penetrate evenly, therefore cooking is not even. Cauliflower and potatoes, on the other hand, allow steam to penetrate right inside — they do not pack as spinach does. Steaming is a slower cooking method than boiling.

Certain vegetables such as broccoli and asparagus have stems and flowers, or stems and tips, or stems and leaves that require a different amount of cooking for the stem to be softened without the rest of it being overdone. The stems and flowers can be separated from one another so that the stems can be put to cook first and the flowers added shortly before they are ready. The amount of cellulose present determines the length of time needed to cook vegetables. Asparagus should be tied in bundles and placed upright in a pan of boiling water with the tips above the level of the water, and cooked until the tips are done.

Possibly it is the Chinese more than any other people who are the most sensitive to the presentation of vegetables, and it is from them we can take an art and culinary lesson in preserving crisp textures, bright colours and the natural flavours of vegetables.

HERBS AND SPICES

The difference between a herb and a spice is that a herb is the fresh or dried green leafy part of a plant, while a spice is the fruit or the bark or the seed of a plant. Both should be bought in very small amounts and kept airtight in a dark jar. Light causes the colour to fade. It is best to allow your collection of herbs and spices to grow as you need them rather than to buy a lot which may not get used immediately. Ideally one should have a fresh lot each year. Spices should be bought whole, that is, whole, not powdered, nutmegs, whole peppercorns, cinnamon bark, coriander seeds, whole cloves, pistils of saffron, and so on. They keep much longer in this way than ground up to a powder. A powder contains air and this allows the flavour and aroma to deteriorate. Ideally you should have a small electric grinder, used purely for spices.

Most herbs and spices are actually incorporated into the dish and eaten. Sometimes they are tied in a muslin bag and removed before serving. A *bouquet garni*, meaning a bunch of herbs, a faggot, is tied with cotton and dangled in the pot while it cooks, and is one that is removed before serving. Certain spices are left whole but are bruised before being added to the dish; bruising or squashing them in this way helps to release the flavour. This method is sometimes used for cardamom pods used in Indian cooking. A bayleaf should not be bruised but can be broken once or twice to get the same effect. Bayleaves, however, are not suited to being ground up.

You will notice in Indian cooking that the ground mixture of herbs, called a *masala*, is fried in fat before the liquids and other ingredients are added. The flavours are thus captured in the oil and are not lost through evaporation. Frying spices also changes their flavour. Herbs, on the other hand, are best added to a long-cooked dish towards the end of cooking so that their impact remains fresh, and they have no chance to become bitter with overcooking.

Some herbs and spices, being far more pungent, have far more effect than others for the same amount. There is not the room here to go into detail regarding each one, however. Be cautious at first: you must never allow the herbs to take over the taste of the dish, unless this is clearly meant to be the case in the recipe you are following. Use fresh herbs wherever possible and let your choice be guided by your own likes and dislikes rather than by hard and fast tradition.

10

Chou-fleur au Gratin and other gratinéed dishes

The word gratin is commonly understood to mean any dish having a cheesy sauce or topping. This is in fact a misnomer, but an understandable one when the general translation of *macaroni au gratin* and *chou-fleur au gratin*, for example, is macaroni cheese and cauliflower cheese. The correct translation of the word *gratin* is the formation of a brown crust. The brown crust is most usually formed by sprinkling a shallow sauced dish with dried or browned breadcrumbs (which may be mixed with grated cheese and more often than not are mixed with grated cheese), and dribbling over with melted butter. The dish is then placed under the grill or in a hot oven until it bubbles around the edges and becomes crisp and golden on top. It should be served immediately.

The word also describes the special dish made for the purpose. It can be earthenware, stoneware, Pyrex or enamelled cast iron and is usually oval in shape, often having ears to each end to facilitate easy removal from the hot oven or grill. It must be shallow. All gratin dishes are shallow so that the food cooks through quickly at the same time as the crust is being nicely browned.

Almost any food can be gratinéed, whether cooked or

from raw. However, when eggs or fish are assembled raw with their sauce, sprinkled with breadcrumbs, possibly with cheese, and dotted or dribbled with butter in the usual way, this constitutes the correct and complete method whereby the food is perfectly cooked at the same instant as the topping is crisp and brown. This has to be done in the oven at a temperature around regulo 4, 180 °C (350 °F). It cannot be successfully cooked under the grill because the food underneath would not be cooked through by the time the top is browned. The second and easier way is to compose the dish with cooked food which is arranged in the dish, masked with a sauce, sprinkled with breadcrumbs and then heated through and browned under the grill or in the oven. Obviously, if the assembled dish has been prepared well in advance and has been allowed to become quite cold, it is better to brown it in the oven where it will get all-round heat. Done under the grill, it may still be cold inside while the top is browned and hot.

Most foods to be gratinéed, whether from raw or cooked, are masked with a sauce — béchamel, cheese and tomato are most popular. However, in some recipes thick fresh cream can replace the sauce; the choice is left to the cook according to suitability, preference and cost. An example is the egg and spinach dish, *oeufs florentines*, which can be made with a béchamel sauce, a cheese sauce or thick cream.

A gratin in which the food has to be cooked from raw (for example, see the recipe for baked stuffed fillets of cod, p. 55) has to be baked at regulo 4 or 5, 180 or 190 °C (350 or 375 °F) for the food to be cooked at the same time as the topping is browned. However, a gratin in which the food has merely to be browned can go into a hot oven, regulo 7, 220 °C (425 °F) or, alternatively, under the grill. It must not be cooked too long or too fast in any event, otherwise the sauce or the cream will curdle. If the cheese topping is to melt slowly and combine with the butter it must not be cooked at such a high temperature either. Whichever way you choose, the dish will bubble up. Allow for this by not filling the gratin dish to the brim in the initial stage, otherwise it will dribble over the sides as it cooks.

The recommended cheeses usually include Parmesan, Emmental or Gruyère, and Cheddar, each for different reasons. Parmesan, in addition to having its own very special flavour, is the only cheese that does not form strings.

Emmental and Gruyère on the other hand become very flowing when heated. Cheddar is an excellent cooking cheese and, of course, is not expensive by comparison.

Food to be gratinéed can be assembled in a pastry shell and so become a *quiche*, rather than cooked in the usual way in a dish. In this case, care must be taken not to scorch the pastry edges.

Cooked pasta, vegetables, ham, eggs, fish, pancakes, even soup, can be gratinéed. They form suitable luncheon and supper dishes and they can be prepared well in advance, requiring little last-minute attention. They include the homely and the sophisticated and there is limitless variation open to the imaginative cook.

CHOU-FLEUR AU GRATIN

Cauliflowerettes masked with a cheese sauce, and browned in the oven or under the grill.

1 large cauliflower; water; salt; For the sauce: 25 g butter; 25 g flour; 275 ml milk; 125 g Cheddar cheese; scant ½ teaspoon made mustard; salt and pepper; For the topping: handful fresh white breadcrumbs; 15 g butter; 2 tomatoes.

Remove the main stem of the cauliflower, then divide into cauliflowerettes. Bring a large saucepan of water to the boil with one dessertspoon of salt. Plunge in the cauliflower and boil, partly covered, for 8 minutes. Drain immediately, then run under cold water for 30 seconds. (This stops the cauliflower cooking in its own residual heat.) Arrange in a gratin dish. Make the sauce by melting the butter in a medium-sized saucepan, then stir in the flour. Cook this *roux* over a moderate heat for a minute or two, using a wooden spoon to stir constantly and without allowing it to brown. Remove from the heat and a little at a time add the milk, stirring well between each addition and the next. When all the milk is used up, return the pan once again to a moderate heat and gently bring to the boil, stirring all the time. As it comes to the boil it will thicken to a coating consistency. Immediately grate the cheese directly into the pan and stir vigorously until it has melted and become smooth again. Stir in the mustard and season with salt and pepper. Mask the cauliflower with this sauce. Make the topping in one of two ways. Either fry the breadcrumbs in the butter until pale gold and scatter over the cauliflower, or scatter the breadcrumbs on first and dot the butter over it. Finally, slice the tomatoes and arrange on the top. Brown under the grill or in the oven at regulo 6, 200 °C (400 °F). [*Serves 3 to 4*]

Note It is important not to cook the cauliflower for longer than necessary for two reasons. First, we do not want it soft and mushy and, secondly, it develops a stronger, undesirable flavour the longer it is cooked.

HOT CHICKEN SALAD

A great little dish. It is easy to prepare, makes a chicken go a long way, is crunchy and tastes good. Popular for informal buffet parties.

2 cupfuls cooked chicken; ½ head celery; 1 small green pepper; 1 medium onion; ½ can concentrated chicken soup; 2 tablespoons mayonnaise; juice of ½ lemon; 1 teaspoon salt; For the topping: 50 g grated Cheddar cheese; 1 cupful chrushed potato crisps.

The amounts of the ingredients are 'more or less'. Cut the chicken into neat pieces. Chop the celery and pepper coarsely and the onion finely. Combine the chicken, vegetables, soup, mayonnaise, lemon juice and salt in a large bowl and stir well. Put the mixture into a gratin dish and smooth over. Make the topping by combining the cheese and crisps and scatter over the dish to cover completely. Bake in a preheated oven at regulo 5, 190 °C (375 °F) for about 20 minutes. Serve hot. [*Serves 4 to 6*]

Hot chicken salad can be prepared well in advance. If you intend preparing it in advance, it is best to soften the onions in a little butter before incorporating them into the mixture so that they do not turn sour. This also makes the taste of onions milder.

GRATIN DAUPHINOIS

Simple, rich and delicious dish of potatoes and cream from the Dauphiné region of France.

> *500 g waxy potatoes; garlic (optional); salt and pepper; 275 ml double cream; 25 g butter; nutmeg.*

Preheat the oven to regulo 3, 170 °C (325 °F). Peel the potatoes and slice into rounds very, very thinly. Keep under cold water to prevent them going brown, then rinse and pat dry. It is essential that the dish to cook them in is shallow, such as a flan dish. Butter the dish then rub into it the cut surface of a clove of garlic if used. Layer the potatoes, seasoning with salt and pepper between the rounds. When they are all used up the potatoes should come nearly to the top of the dish. Pour in the cream. Brush with the melted butter and dust with a grating of nutmeg. Bake for 1½ hours, turning the oven up high towards the very end to brown the top. *Gratin dauphinois* can be served as a first course to a meal. It can also accompany a plain roast or grilled meat.

[*Serves 4*]

Note Some recipes advocate eggs and Gruyère cheese in this dish but this is the essential one and none the less lovely for that. The method whereby a mere *hint* of garlic can be introduced into a dish such as this where a stronger flavour is not wanted can also be used in the preparation of a salad: the salad bowl is smeared with the juice from a cut clove of garlic rubbed round the inside before the vegetables are added.

HAM IN CREAM SAUCE

Rolls of thinly sliced ham with mushrooms, thick cream and Parmesan cheese browned in the oven or under the grill.

> *1 large onion; 3 fresh or canned tomatoes; ½ bottle dry white wine or cider; 8 to 12 thin slices cooked ham; 125 g mushrooms; 25 g butter; 1 teaspoon*

flour; 275 ml double cream; salt and pepper; 25 g Parmesan cheese.

Chop the onions finely and put with the tomatoes and wine or cider into a small saucepan. Bring to the boil, then simmer uncovered until the liquid is reduced to 1 tablespoon. Meanwhile, roll up each slice of ham and arrange down the centre of a gratin dish. Wipe clean the mushrooms, then slice. Heat the butter in a frying pan, toss in the mushrooms and sauté until brown. Scatter over the ham. Blend the flour with the cream. Sieve the tomatoes and mushrooms, pressing out as much juice as possible. Add this concentrated liquor to the cream and heat gently in a saucepan, stirring as you do so. Season. As it comes to the boil, remove from the heat and mask the ham and mushrooms. Sprinkle with the Parmesan cheese. Either brown in a hot oven, regulo 7, 220 °C (425 °F) or under the grill. If the dish has been allowed to go completely cold, brown in a moderate oven, regulo 4, 180 °C (350 °F) to ensure that it is completely heated through. Do not heat for too long, otherwise the sauce will separate. Serve with boiled potatoes. [*Serves 4 to 6*]

CHEESY LEEKS AND HAM

8 thin leeks; water; salt; 8 thin slices cooked ham; For the cheese sauce: 25 g butter; 25 g flour; 275 ml milk; 125 g Cheddar cheese; ½ teaspoon made mustard; salt and pepper; For the topping: handful fresh white breadcrumbs; 15 g butter; 2 tomatoes.

Trim the leeks and wash carefully (soil tends to lodge between the layers). Put water and salt in a large saucepan sufficient to just cover the leeks. Bring to the boil, drop the leeks in and cook uncovered for 10 minutes. Remove immediately and drain. (If the dish is not to be completed straight away the leeks can be rinsed under cold water to stop them cooking in the residual heat.) Roll each leek in a slice of ham and arrange in a gratin dish. Meanwhile make the sauce. Melt the butter carefully in a medium-sized saucepan, stir in the flour and cook for a minute or two without browning, stirring constantly with a wooden spoon. Remove from the heat. A little at a time to start with add the milk, stirring well between additions until it is smooth and all used up. You should now have a lump-free but thin sauce. Return once more to the heat and gently bring to the boil, stirring all the time. Remove from the heat and grate the cheese directly into it while still very hot. Stir vigorously until the cheese melts and the sauce becomes smooth again. Stir in the mustard and season with salt and pepper. Mask the leeks and ham with this. Scatter the breadcrumbs over and dot with butter. Slice the tomatoes and arrange over the top. Brown under the grill or in a hot oven at regulo 7, 220 °C (425 °F). If the dish is allowed to go cold first, brown in a moderate oven at regulo 4, 180 °C (350 °F) to make sure it is heated right through. [*Serves 4*]

Note A quick method of making a basic white sauce (to which grated cheese is added to make a cheese sauce) is simply to put the milk, flour and butter all at once into a saucepan, whisk to remove the lumps of flour, then heat the lump-free but thin liquid to melt the butter and burst the starch grains in the flour. It is when the starch grains swell and burst, as they do in a hot liquid, that the liquid becomes thick. You must stir all the time.

The advantage of the roux method (described elsewhere in this book for making white and cheese sauces) is said to be that the initial cooking of the flour and butter ensures that the flour is well cooked and prevents the sauce tasting starchy. However, I have done some comparisons and cannot detect any difference in flavour between sauces made by either method.

11

Rognons Sauté and other sautéed dishes

The word *sauté* literally translated means to jump. Small pieces of food cooked in very hot fat sizzle and thus seem to jump as they are siezed at the high temperature required for this kind of cooking. The equivalent in English cooking is shallow frying, while the Chinese methods of quick-frying and stir-frying are perfect demonstrations of its real meaning. There is, however, some misunderstanding regarding the meaning of sauté. Is it a complete method of cooking in itself or merely a preliminary step whereby food is sealed and browned before being cooked further by some other method? The original interpretation is to fully cook tender pieces of meat in hot fat. It has since also come to mean a preliminary step in the making of casseroles and so on. It can also mean a method whereby additional flavour and colour are given to vegetables already cooked, for example, sauté potatoes.

The utensil to use is a *sautoir* or a frying pan. A real *sautoir* is somewhat deeper than the usual frying pan. The pan should have a base that is reasonably heavy but not so heavy that it makes tossing the food difficult. The pan should be big enough to hold the food in one layer but not so big that the juices dry up and burn round the edge. Foods suited to being sautéed include kidneys, livers, sweetbreads, small pieces of firm fish, small pieces of fillet steak, entrecôte and cutlets. The smaller the pieces, the more quickly will they cook through. It is important that all the pieces are of equal size, however, so that they cook uniformly. There would otherwise be an unsatisfactory mixture of underdone, overdone and nicely done pieces of food.

A sauté is made by cooking the food in hot fat, tossing the food around to cook evenly on all sides, then removing it to the warmed serving dish, keeping it warm while the pan juices are deglazed with stock or wine, which are reduced and poured over the food to serve. This is the basic method and you will usually find more elaborate recipes. It is a method requiring constant attention, quick execution and a certain amount of skill. It needs practice before consistency is achieved. Its very urgency demands that the table is laid, the diners assembled and everything else is got ready for the meal before it is begun. Once cooked the dish has to be eaten immediately to be enjoyed to the full. Unlike casseroles and gratin dishes it cannot be prepared in advance to be reheated or left in the oven to look after itself.

Any sauté served with a sauce should not be swimming in it, but the pieces of food should be just masked. It is usual to stir in a small knob of chilled butter at the last minute to give the finished sauce a good gloss. Do not continue to cook after it is added.

One of the nice things about sautéed dishes is that they can quickly and easily be geared to cooking for one or two persons. There are so many dishes in cookery that cannot be tailored down or which take so much time that they are not worth the effort when cooking for one or two. In fact, sautéed dishes are best suited to small amounts of food. They become unmanageable otherwise.

ROGNONS SAUTÉ

Tender pieces of kidney fried quickly in butter with bacon, flamed with brandy.

450 g lambs' kidneys; 25 g butter; 1 tablespoon oil; 4 rashers streaky bacon; small glass brandy; salt and pepper.

It is likely that the kidneys are trimmed of fat and skin when you buy them. Inside each one is a whitish core which should be clipped away with a pair of scissors, or use a sharp knife. Slice each kidney into four or five pieces. Set aside. In a frying pan heat the butter and oil over a low heat until the butter melts. Swirl the pan around so that the butter does not brown around the edges. Meanwhile, remove the rind from the bacon. Chop the bacon finely. Assemble the kidneys and bacon together. All of it must be perfectly dry, as should all foods to be sautéed. Turn up the heat under the pan and, when the butter begins to foam, toss in the kidneys and bacon, shaking the pan around as you do so. It should sizzle. Continue to shake the pan in order to toss the pieces of meat so that they cook evenly on all sides. If you find it easier, use a wooden spoon to turn the kidneys over. After a minute, test a piece for tenderness and see also that the redness has gone. Pour the brandy in one side of the pan, then tip towards the flame and ignite. Alternatively, use a lighted match. Allow the flames to subside, season the dish and serve. If liked, a little double cream may be stirred into the kidneys just prior to serving. Plain boiled rice would accompany this simple dish well. [*Serves 3 to 4*]

Note Food can be sautéed in almost any fat, depending on the flavour you want or depending on what you have available at the time. It can be butter, oil, lard, margarine or cleaned dripping. Recipes frequently call for a mixture of butter and oil. This combines the advantages of both. Butter gives good colour and flavour but burns very easily. Oil, on the other hand, has a very high burning point, so that the combined fats can be raised to a higher temperature than butter on its own could without risk of burning. If butter is to be used alone it should be clarified. This gets rid of the salts which rise to the top in a creamy foam when butter is heated and are the cause of butter burning quickly.

SAUTÉED SWEETBREADS

Done in the Italian way with Marsala.

450 g lambs' sweetbreads; water; salt; lemon or vinegar; 4 rashers lean smoked bacon; 25 g butter; 1 tablespoon oil; 75 ml Marsala; pinch sage; salt and pepper.

Cut the sweetbreads into small nuggets, removing bits of fat and skin if necessary. Put them into a bowl of cold water with a teaspoon of salt and a little lemon or vinegar (about 15 ml). Set aside for 30 minutes. (This method draws out the last traces of blood and helps keep them white.) Remove the rind from the bacon and chop finely. Carefully melt the butter and oil in a frying pan over a gentle heat, swirling it around so as not to allow it to brown around the edges. Meanwhile, pat the sweetbreads dry on kitchen paper. Turn up the heat under the pan and when the butter begins to foam toss in the sweetbreads and bacon, shaking the pan as you do so to turn the pieces over and cook them evenly on all sides. Use a wooden spoon if you find it easier. When all pinkish traces have gone from the sweetbreads, test to see if a piece is tender—if it is, then it is done. Lambs' sweetbreads should only take a few minutes. When done, pour the Marsala over the sweetbreads and allow to bubble and reduce until thick and syrupy. Scatter in the sage and season. Serve immediately. [*Serves 4*]

Note As for all sautéed dishes, the food must be dry before you put it into the fat. If it is put in wet there would first be a lot of spitting from the pan, over the cook and the cooker; secondly, a steamy layer would be formed between the meat and the hot fat and the meat would not be sealed the instant it should be, resulting in loss of juices; also, fat would be absorbed, making the food soggy. It is important to have the fat very hot and to have enough hot fat to cover the base of the pan by ¼ cm. If there is too little the food will stick, too much and it makes it impossible to toss the food over. Being able to toss the food in the professional manner demands practice. Most people are happy using a wooden spoon and make less mess.

LIVER WITH DUBONNET AND ORANGE

Thin slices of tender lamb's liver, briefly sautéed, and removed to a warm serving plate while the pan juices are deglazed and made into a sauce with the liquor and fruit juice.

> *1 medium-sized onion; 1 clove garlic; 1 tablespoon olive oil; 50 g butter; 450 g lamb's liver; 25 g or more seasoned flour; juice 1 small orange; 100 ml red Dubonnet; 2 tablespoons finely chopped parsley; grated rind of ½ orange; 1 teaspoon grated lemon rind; For garnish: finely chopped parsley; grated orange rind.*

Have all the ingredients and the garnish ready assembled before proceeding to cook. Slice the onion and cut the garlic into slices also (that is, do not mash). Measure the oil and butter into a large frying pan. Slice the liver thinly and evenly then dust in the seasoned flour both sides, shaking off any excess. Set aside. Combine the orange juice and Dubonnet in a small jug. Combine the chopped parsley and the grated rinds of orange and lemon on a saucer. (The lemon should be grated on the very fine edge of the grater and the orange rind on a less fine edge.) Prepare the garnish. Now proceed to cook the dish by firstly softening the onion and garlic in the melted fat; this takes about 10 minutes. Meanwhile, put a suitable serving plate to keep warm. Using a slotted spoon, remove the onion and garlic, pressing out the juices as you do so. You only require the fat which is now flavoured with the imparted flavours of the aromatics. Turn the heat up high and when the fat starts to foam add the pieces of liver to sit comfortably side by side. Shake the pan to prevent the liver sticking to it. Turn the heat down to moderate. When the blood begins to rise, use a pair of tongs to turn the pieces over and do the other side. It will take only a few minutes either side — the degree is a matter of choice since some people like the blood to actually run from the liver they eat. Prolonged cooking makes liver tough. Remove to the warmed serving plate. Tip the liquor (orange and Dubonnet) into the pan and deglaze, using a wooden spoon to scrape all the bits from the bottom and sides. Reduce until thick and syrupy.

Finally, stir in the parsley and the grated rinds and mask the pieces of liver with this sauce. Garnish by scattering the dish with more parsley and the grated rind of orange. Serve immediately. [*Serves 4*]

Note It is essential to use tongs for turning the pieces of liver because if you poke them with a fork all the juices run out. This also applies when grilling or frying meat.

KIDNEY AND SAUSAGE TURBIGO

With the addition of tomato and onions this dish has a sweetish tang which is very appealing. It suits those people who find kidneys on their own too strong.

> *15 g lard; 2 large sausages; 1 onion; 225 g lambs' kidneys; 15 g flour; 1 tablespoon tomato ketchup; 275 ml chicken stock; ½ teaspoon thyme; salt and pepper.*

Melt the lard in a large frying pan and in it gently cook the sausages until browned on all sides. Meanwhile, slice the onion and prepare the kidneys. Remove the whitish core from the centre of each kidney using a pair of scissors or a sharp knife. Cut each kidney into five or six pieces. Remove the sausages from the pan and set aside until cooled and firm enough to handle. In the fat that remains in the pan gently sauté the onions until golden brown. Add the kidneys to the onions, and continue to cook, shaking the pan as you do so or use a wooden spoon to turn the kidneys over and over. You should attend to them constantly. After a few minutes or when there are no longer any pinkish traces remaining in the kidney, toss in the flour and cook, stirring as you do so for a further minute or two. Add the tomato ketchup and the stock and allow to come gently to the boil, stirring constantly. Turn the heat down to simmer. Slice the now cooled sausages into rounds and add to the kidneys. Add the thyme and season. Test a piece of kidney to see if it is tender. If it is not, continue cooking a little while longer until done. Serve with plain boiled rice. [*Serves 2 to 3*]

12

Pastry

There is possibly no other area of cookery in which the touch of the cook's hands is as important as it is in pastrymaking. Some pastries need a light touch while another requires bold kneading. The ability to make good pastry eludes many people. They may eventually give up and assume that they do not possess the secret knack. There is no secret, but there are a few facts to be learned about flour itself, which is the chief substance of pastry. We need to know what happens when flour is crumbled with fat, and when it is mixed with water, and to realise the important effect that handling has on the dough. An irreversible change takes place in the structure of the dough when it is handled or kneaded; in certain pastries this is desirable while for others it would be disastrous. We need to ask whether the temperature of the ingredients has any bearing and why it is necessary to rest some pastries in the refrigerator before rolling out — is this a vital step to success?

It is in the comparison of two very diverse kinds of pastry, shortcrust and the less common strudel dough, that a student can be made to appreciate the qualities and possibilities of good fresh flour. He will be amazed to learn how four ingredients — flour, fat, water and egg — can be made into two totally different products: a short, crumbly one that is a little difficult to manage because for the beginner it breaks or cracks or sticks to the table, and strudel dough, which is smooth and so elastic that it can be made to stretch until it is as thin as tissue paper, and become so thin that a letter laid underneath can easily be read through.

The explanation starts by understanding the protein in flour which is called gluten, and this is the stuff which, when mixed with a liquid and then kneaded, becomes elastic and tough — very necessary in the making of strudel dough. (If this pastry were not made as thin as tissue paper and rolled up with lots of butter inside it would be so hard as to be quite impossible to eat.) In shortcrust pastry, on the other hand, kneading, indeed any unnecessary handling, is to be avoided at all costs to produce the pastry required; if you fail to observe this the dough will lose its loose crumbly nature and will become pliable and far more easy to handle than it should. If this happens there is unfortunately no remedy, but you will have to start again with fresh ingredients. To produce good shortcrust dough demanding great care in handling and then in rolling out should mark a big personal achievement to the novice cook since there is far more to the deceptively simple looking piecrust than meets the eye.

The amount of water in a dough also affects the gluten: the more water there is the more it will become elastic. It is clear therefore that the amount of water in shortcrust pastry should be kept to a minimum, sufficient only to bind the other ingredients together and no more. Excess water in shortcrust pastry makes it hard. Another factor that affects the gluten is temperature. Recipes may instruct you to use iced water for mixing and may even suggest using a glass rolling pin filled with iced water. The reason for keeping everything as cool as possible is twofold. A dough made with cold crumbly fat and flour contains more air than if it is allowed to become oily and therefore heavy. (Light shortcrust pastry is not a result of using self-raising flour as some people believe but comes partly from the use of cool ingredients and partly from the way they are handled.) The second reason for using cold or iced water is that it delays gluten development. Yet another way of delaying or stopping gluten development is by rubbing fat into the flour so that the fat coats the strands, causing them to slide by each other rather than pulling against one another. A rich shortcrust (containing more fat) is much more crumbly and short than a leaner one for the reason just described. However, it is possible to go too far with the amount of fat used and the degree to which it is rubbed into shortcrust pastry. If too much is rubbed in for too long so that it becomes oily looking and turns a dark yellow, the dough may fail to adhere altogether, having been made excessively short.

Before examining in detail the methods for making pastry, note that only dough that has been kneaded to make it elastic should, indeed must, be rested in the refrigerator before it is used or while it is in the process of being made; these doughs are strudel dough, pasta dough, *pâte brisée*, puff and rough puff pastry dough. The effect of resting in the refrigerator is that it relaxes the dough, making it extensible and enabling you to roll it out, and where necessary to stretch it easily, which would otherwise not be the case. Although puff pastry by nature is not meant to stretch, it is rolled and folded and consequently 'worked' so hard that it becomes toughened in the process and has to be rested several times in the making so that it can easily be rolled again. Another point is that if you fail to observe this there is a good chance that the butter will start oozing through.

SHORTCRUST

Most commonly made 'everyday' pastry, suitable for pie-crusts, tarts and flan cases. Its few ingredients make it seem deceptively simple, however. Rich shortcrust and sweet shortcrust pastry follow the same principles and contain more fat, additional egg and sugar.

> *125 g all-purpose white flour; large pinch salt; 30 g butter; 30 g lard; 1 to 2 tablespoons water to mix.*

It is important to use fresh flour, not more than 6 months old, of good quality. Flour that has deteriorated does not cohere but breaks up when rolled out or lifted.

Put the flour and salt into a large mixing bowl. Cut up the fat (butter and lard) and drop them into the flour. Use the tips of the first two fingers and the thumb of each hand to rub the lumps of fat into the flour. (The action is the same as that meaning 'money'.) Lift the mixture above the bowl so that the crumbs fall back, taking air into the mixture at the same time; this will help to make the pastry lighter. On no account should the warm palms of your hands be used, otherwise the mixture will become oily. The mixture to achieve should resemble fine breadcrumbs and be light in colour, crumbly and still floury. If you overdo things at this stage the colour will become dark yellow and the mixture will look oily. Have a palette knife, a tablespoon and a jug of cold water at hand. Now add 1 tablespoon of water to the flour mixture and use the palette knife to stir and cut it in. If after about 10 seconds it still looks very dry and floury, add a further half tablespoon and continue the chopping action with the knife. If you now have sufficient water, the dough will have started to form big lumps and there will be little loose flour around the edge of the bowl. At this stage, use the fingertips only to gather it into a dough. Do not handle it any further — there should be no kneading — no squeezing, nothing. The pastry can now be rolled out and used immediately.

Note This pastry can be made using almost any kind or combination of fats, that is, all lard, all butter, all margarine, all dripping or a mixture of these. The choice is purely a matter of taste according to the colour, the flavour and the texture each gives. It can be seen that ordinary shortcrust pastry is made with half the weight of fat to flour. A richer dough could be made using up to 70 g of fat to 125 g of flour. A rich dough, being more crumbly, is a little more difficult to handle.

It is not really possible to be precise about the amount of water to use, since so much depends on the temperature of the ingredients and of the utensils and the room. In effect it is as *little* as is required to bind the mixture lightly and easily together. It is a mistake to try to press the mixture into a dough before it has been adequately chopped and mixed with the knife. Too much water will make the pastry hard.

Rolling Out Shortcrust Pastry

A dusting of flour is needed to prevent the pastry sticking to the table and rolling pin. It is not necessary to use a pastry board provided you have a smooth and clean working surface. A Formica top is ideal. Lightly dust the surface with flour and lay the lump of pastry down. Never dust the pastry with flour or allow any to fall into the cracks at this stage. Use the hands to carefully pat the dough into a squat square or a round shape, corresponding to the eventual shape you want it to become. Pinch the small cracks around the edge together, otherwise these will become bigger cracks later when rolling out. Dust the rolling pin with flour and before actually doing any rolling out depress the pastry at short intervals to make it thinner and larger. Turn the pastry round and do the same. When you have patted the dough to a thickness of 1½ to 2 cm, start to roll it out. This is *not* done by rolling from one end of the pastry to the other. Roll the rolling pin forwards and backwards in one movement, 5 to 7 cm each way *once*, then lift the rolling pin right off the dough. Thus it never rolls over and over. The rolling movement with this kind of pastry is short and sharp. Before repeating this action, turn the pastry round. It is important to keep the pastry on the move all the time between rollings, so swish some flour remaining on the table underneath it as you turn it round. In this way you can be certain it is not sticking to the table. Always turn the pastry round, not yourself! Never turn the pastry over, otherwise more flour will be rolled in and the proportions will be altered, making it hard. As the pastry becomes bigger, you will need to roll it several times before turning the pastry round. Also, as the pastry becomes bigger it is increasingly more difficult to manipulate. To get it from the table to the pie-dish simply flop it over the rolling pin, then lift the rolling pin with the pastry hanging over to where you want it to be.

Glazing and Baking

The surface of a pie will become brown and shiny if it is brushed with beaten egg before it is baked. It is only savoury pies that should be glazed. Fruit tarts should be baked plain, then dusted with caster sugar or icing sugar to serve. If they are dusted too soon from the oven with icing sugar, however, the heat will melt the sugar and the effect is lost. Most baked goods made with shortcrust pastry should go into a regulo 5, 190 °C (375 °F) oven for at least 30 minutes.

APPLE STRUDEL

An Austrian speciality. The pastry is stretched in the hands and becomes so thin it should be possible to read handwriting through it. However, it is easier to make than it sounds.

1 egg; 1 tablespoon oil; 60 ml water; 150 g strong white flour; pinch salt; For filling: 75 g butter; 75 g white breadcrumbs; 125 g brown sugar; 25 g sultanas; 1 level teaspoon cinnamon; grated rind of one lemon; 25 g walnuts; 5 cooking apples; For topping: egg wash; 50 g whole almonds; icing sugar.

Beat together the egg, oil and water in a small basin. Mix the flour and salt in a large bowl and make a hollow in the centre. Pour in the liquids and beat hard with a wooden spoon until a dough is formed. Add a little more flour if necessary — the dough should be soft and pliable. Turn on to a floured surface and knead for 10 minutes, taking care not to introduce more flour than is needed to stop it sticking. Wrap in a polythene bag and allow to rest in the refrigerator for at least 30 minutes. Preheat the oven to regulo 5, 190 °C (375 °F). Spread two clean tea towels or a piece of sheeting over a large table and dust well with flour. Roll out the rested dough to about the size of a dinner plate. Now flour the hands and, starting in the middle of the dough, pull it gently over outstretched fingers. Aim for a rectangle measuring 1 m long by ¾ m wide. This stretching sounds difficult, but you will soon get the hang of it, and it is great fun to do. Start to make up the strudel by first melting the butter and brushing it over the whole surface of the pastry. For the filling sprinkle the breadcrumbs over one-third of the dough at one end. Likewise sprinkle the sugar, sultanas, cinnamon and grated rind of the lemon on top of the breadcrumbs. Chop the walnuts and add. Peel and core the apples and grate them directly on to the rest of the filling. Place a large baking sheet under the cloth at the opposite end of the filling. Trim the edges of the pastry all round. Working from the filling end, take up the cloth in each corner using each hand, and roll towards the tray, causing the strudel to roll up swiss-roll fashion as you do so. The strudel should end up draped over the tray and then you can completely remove the cloth. Bring the two ends of the strudel round to meet each other, forming a circle (you may need to trim the ends to achieve a neat fit). Brush the top and sides with beaten egg. Blanch the almonds and cut into shreds. Press them over the strudel to make them stick on the egg. Bake for approximately 30 minutes or until the top is golden brown. If necessary, cover the strudel with a sheet of greaseproof paper for the last 15 minutes of baking to prevent the almonds becoming too brown. Allow the strudel to become warm, then dust with icing sugar. Slide on to a serving plate and serve. [*Serves 8*]

Note If you bake the strudel on the back of the baking sheet, turning it upside down, it is easy to slide it straight off and on to the serving plate without risk of breaking. Note that the apples are grated rather than cut into pieces since in this way they cook more quickly and they do not poke through the thin pastry as pieces of apple might. In some recipes, the ingredients are all mixed together in a bowl first before being spread on to the pastry, but I prefer to do it as I have just described because no two mouthfuls then taste exactly the same and it is more interesting to the palate, for example, one mouthful might be a bit more lemony while another might have more spice or walnut in it.

PÂTE BRISÉE

A pastry traditionally made by the French which is suited to the making of flan cases, being crisper and firmer than short-crust, which tends to crumble. You can make it directly on a clean table top or, if you think you might make too much mess, use a large mixing bowl in the usual way.

125 g flour; pinch of salt; 60 g softened butter; 1 egg; ½ to 1 tablespoon water.

Pile the flour and salt in a mound directly on to the working surface. Make a hollow in the middle of the flour and put in the butter, cut up in pieces, and the whole egg. Use the fingertips of one hand to mix these ingredients together, using a kind of pinching action and trying to get the ingredients evenly mixed. The ingredients may form a dough without the addition of any water, otherwise use a very small amount of water to form a dough. If too much is used the pastry will be hard when it is baked. Use the heel of the hand to press this dough into a round about the size of a saucer. Fold the saucer in half, then in half again. Repeat this action twice more: it will make the pastry have flaky layers because of the folding you have just done. Allow the pastry to relax in the refrigerator for 20 minutes before using to make a flan case.

CHOUX PASTRY

Choux, meaning cabbages, which is what puffed up choux buns are meant to resemble. This pastry is also used for chocolate éclairs, profiteroles and *gougère*.

> *150 ml water; 45 g butter; 70 g strong white flour; pinch salt; 2 eggs.*

Bring the water and butter to the boil in a medium-sized saucepan. Meanwhile, weigh the flour ready and add the salt. Beat the eggs in a small basin. As soon as the water comes to the boil and the butter is melted and bubbling, shoot in the flour all at once and beat hard with a wooden spoon. The paste thus formed should leave the inside of the pan clean. (If it fails to form a paste, return the saucepan to the heat and beat hard until it does.) Remove and allow to cool for several minutes. Beat in the egg. If the egg is added too soon it will cook in the heat and the pastry will not rise—2 minutes' wait should be about right. Stand the saucepan on a damp dishcloth to stop it sliding around the table while you add the egg. The egg should be added a little at a time and beaten well between additions. It needs a little patience. When nearly all the egg is used up consider whether the last spoonful will make the paste you have into a semi-liquid or whether you think it will remain a stiff paste that holds its shape—which is how it should be. If you add too much egg the pastry will not work for you. The amount is never quite the same because sometimes the eggs are slightly bigger or smaller than the previous time, or your weighing out may not have been spot-on accurate. Use this pastry as required. Items made with choux pastry should be put into a regulo 7, 220 °C (425 °C) oven on the middle shelf for the first 20 minutes, then reduced to regulo 5, 190 °C (375 °F) for a further 20 minutes, making 40 minutes in all.

People are sometimes caught out over the cooking, because although the pastry will be risen and golden brown after 20 minutes, it is not risen *and* set firm, so that when it is removed from the oven and cools it flops down. The golden brown colour of choux pastry not long after it has been in the oven often deceives people into thinking that it is done. When making éclairs or choux buns, after 35 minutes or when firm they should be split and laid open on the baking sheet and returned again to the oven, now lowered to regulo 3, 170 °C (325 °F) to dry out for just a few more minutes.

PUFF PASTRY

450 g white flour; 1 level teaspoon salt; 275 ml cold water; juice 1 lemon; 350 g butter.

It is essential that you give yourself a span of approximately 3 hours to make this pastry so that it can relax adequately between rollings out. If you hurry it, the pastry is tough and difficult to manipulate. If you take the proper time the pastry rolls out easily and will be successful.

Put the flour and salt into a large mixing bowl and make a hollow in the middle. Combine the water and lemon juice and add *all at once* to the flour. Use a wooden spoon to quickly incorporate the flour and liquid so that it all gets mixed at once. Turn the dough on to a floured surface and knead until smooth. It will now be tough and elastic and must be allowed to rest for 30 minutes to relax, after which it can easily be rolled out. Put the dough to rest wrapped in a polythene bag in the refrigerator. Meanwhile, prepare the butter. The butter has to be cool and soft rather than cool and hard. Since it is to be incorporated into the dough in one piece, the consistency of the two should be equal. If the butter is very hard, it will poke through the layers of dough and become impossible to handle. To make the butter soft use the butter straight from the refrigerator and place it on a large double thickness of greaseproof paper. Fold the paper over to cover it and use a rolling pin to beat it into a softened rectangle about the size of a small sheet of notepaper. If it goes into an odd shape, cut pieces off and patch it up to get a good shape. Set aside. Roll the now rested dough into the shape shown in figure 12.1*a*, allowing it to be thicker in the middle. The size should be three times bigger each way than the butter. Place the butter in the middle of the dough (figure 12.1*b*). Fold the bottom third of pastry up and over the butter to completely cover it. Press gently down, trying not to tear the dough. Damp the edges, so that when you

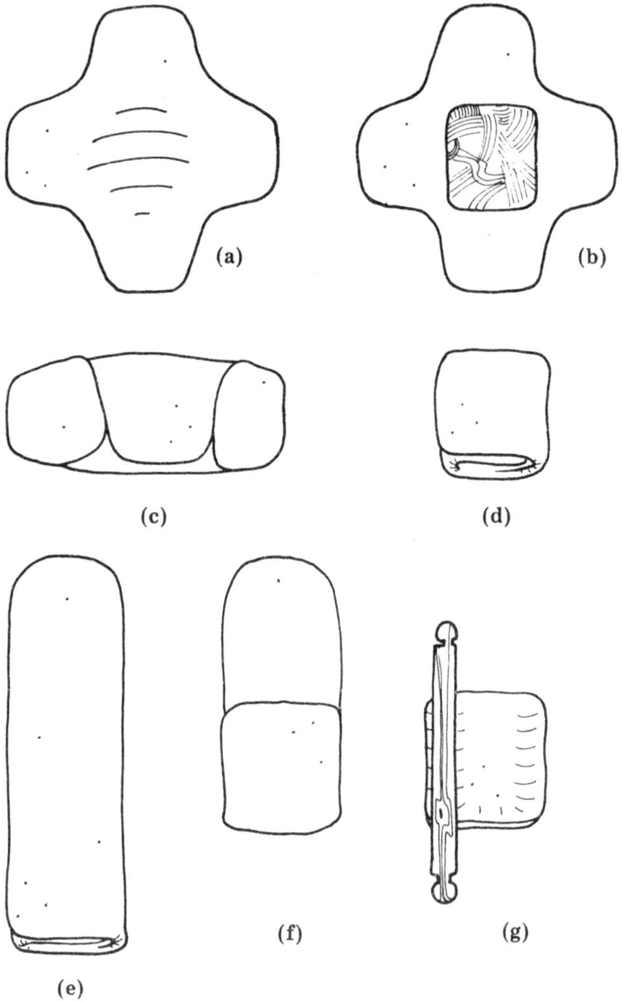

Figure 12.1 How to make puff pastry

next fold the top third of pastry down over the first fold, it can be firmly sealed (figure 12.1*c*). Repeat this process in exactly the same way sideways (figure 12.1*d*). Use the side of the rolling pin to press and seal the edges. Roll the pastry out to a large rectangle three times longer than it is wide (figure 12.1*e*). Aim to keep a good rectangular shape. The next rolling and folding process has to be repeated five more times — but not all at once. Fold the bottom third of the pastry up (figure 12.1*f*) and the top third down (figure 12.1*g*), carefully brushing with a little water to seal the edges as you do so. Repeat a second time. Cover with polythene and place in the refrigerator to rest for ½ hour. Replace the pastry on the floured surface in front of you, having given it a quarter turn from the way it was. Twice more repeat the last rolling and folding process. Allow it to rest covered in the refrigerator for another ½ hour. Twice more roll and fold, giving a quarter turn between operations. Finally allow to rest another ½ hour before using. The pastry has now been rolled and folded six times in all.

All puff pastry, no matter for what purpose, should be placed in a preheated regulo 8, 230 °C (450 °F) oven for the first 10 minutes, which should then be lowered to regulo 6, 200 °C (400 °F) for the remainder of the cooking time. See additional notes on puff pastry on pp. 157–9.

Note Notice that the proportion of fat to flour is ¾ : 1 in weight and not equal, as in some recipes. Pastry made with equal quantities drips butter as it bakes.

ROUGH PUFF PASTRY

Very quick to prepare in contrast to the real puff pastry.

> *250 g plain flour; ½ level teaspoon salt; 150 g frozen otherwise very cold butter; water to mix.*

Mix the flour and salt in a large bowl. Grate the butter coarsely into it. Alternatively, the butter can be cut into small dice and the dice mixed in with the flour. You should toss the butter into the flour as you add it, otherwise it will pile up and stick together in a big lump. Use a round-bladed knife to mix in the water — up to 6 tablespoons — to form a soft dough. Dust a clean working surface lightly with flour and roll out the dough to a rectangle measuring 15 cm by 45 cm. Fold the bottom third of the pastry upwards and the top third downwards so that you now have a square measuring 15 cm. Give the pastry a quarter turn so that the open ends are towards you. Repeat this rolling out and folding process twice more, making three times in all. Wrap the pastry in polythene and allow it to relax in the refrigerator for 20 minutes before using. A pie having this pastry as its crust should normally be baked in a preheated hot oven, regulo 8, 230 °C (450 °F) for 10 minutes, reducing the temperature to regulo 6, 200 °C (400 °F) for the remainder of the cooking time, which will be about 20 minutes, making 30 minutes in all. However, you should cook it according to your recipe since some fillings may take longer to cook than 30 minutes, particularly if they are raw to start with.

HOT-WATER CRUST PASTRY

As used for raised pies. Sugar is used in this recipe, which sounds odd, but tastes right.

> *575 g plain flour; 2 rounded teaspoons salt; 1 rounded tablespoon icing sugar; 250 g lard; 200 ml water.*

Put the flour, salt and sugar into a large mixing bowl and make a hollow in the middle. Bring the lard and water to the boil, then pour immediately into the hollow and beat with a wooden spoon. A paste will be formed which is partly cooked from the heat of the liquid. It is very malleable and must be used while warm. If it is allowed to cool it becomes hard and is impossible to use. Hot water crust is not rolled out to fit but is pushed into and up the sides of the mould with the knuckles. If holes appear they can easily be patched. (See recipe for veal-and-ham pie on p. 42.)

PASTA

The commercial variety is not a patch on home-made pasta. Home-made pasta has a soft texture, tastes really good and is great fun to prepare. Serve plain-boiled with salt, freshly ground black pepper, butter and freshly grated Parmesan cheese.

8 heaped tablespoons strong white flour (225 g); 1 level teaspoon salt; 1 egg; 1 teaspoon oil; approximately 4 tablespoons water.

Pile the flour and salt on to a clean working surface and make a hollow in the middle. Add the egg and the oil to the hollow. Using the fingertips of one hand start to pinch the egg and flour together, adding a sprinkling of water as you do so. It will take you about 5 minutes of pinching before you have a pile of doughy 'shreds' in front of you. You should now be able to use the whole of your hand to gather these up and form a fairly dry dough. Knead using the heel of your hand. You will have to stand up to do this so that you can put your weight on it. When the dough is smooth cut it in half and flatten each piece. Wrap in a polythene bag and put it to relax for 30 minutes in the refrigerator, after which it will have softened and be easy to roll out. If a pasta machine is not being used make *tagliatelle* (ribbons) in the following way. Lightly flour the work surface, place one piece of dough on it and start to roll it out in a length. You will notice that this is fairly hard to do and also that the dough springs back. After you have rolled it out to about 25 cm, wrap it around the rolling pin, stretching it around the rolling pin as you do so. Leave it like this for a few minutes, after which, when you unravel it, it will no longer shrink back. If you have a second rolling pin or an empty bottle at hand, you can prepare the second piece in the same way. Proceed with rolling, stretching and wrapping around the rolling pin until the pastry is so thin that you can just begin to see through it. Roll one length of the pasta dough up like a Swiss-roll. Use a sharp knife to cut sections of ½ cm. Unravel these 'catherine wheels' and drape over the back of a chair or a towel rail. They have to be separated in this way to prevent them from sticking together. Pasta is best cooked fresh. These 'ribbons' will take about 7 minutes to cook in a large pan of salted boiling water, after which you drain them, return them to the empty pan with a large knob of butter and swirl them around. Serve with more butter, black pepper and Parmesan cheese. If the freshly made pasta is not for immediate consumption, you can allow the ribbons to dry out completely and store them until required. Dry them overnight by laying the ribbons side by side in one layer on a clean teatowel. [*Serves 4*]

13

How to Make Bread

The requirements of a good loaf start with the ingredients: good quality yeast, the right kind of flour and the correct amount of salt and water. The second requirement is a cook who understands exactly what is going on in the process. It is not usually sufficient simply to follow the recipe. Yeast dough is a lump of very sensitive living material, reacting this way and that to the conditions we provide. The cook needs to know what to do, for example, if the yeast fails to 'sponge' in the recommended time, and why; how to tell when loaves are proved or if they are overproved; how to test whether a loaf is nicely cooked, and so on.

In the home kitchen, consistent results are nearly impossible to achieve. Every loaf will look different, but will always have the same delicious smell and a lovely crust of brown. There are few people who cannot be tempted by home-made bread and, having made it once, are not charmed by the way it totally involves the person making it. Some people assert that the ability to make good bread is a gift, like the ability to paint. But it stems really from the simple awareness that yeast has a life and a will of its own, and that without due respect to this, both the yeast and the cook are certain to fail from the start.

This living plant reacts to temperature, to moisture, to salt and, in the making of rich doughs (teacakes, doughnuts, etc.), to the additional ingredients of sugar, fruit and fat. It can, however, react so violently against what is done to it by an unsuspecting cook that it can literally die and be rendered useless as a raising agent.

The cook's job is to provide optimum growth conditions for the yeast in the initial stages: moisture, food in the form of flour, and warmth. The yeast produces air bubbles within the dough during this time and it is these that expand, acting as the raising agent and making the bread light. The bread is baked in a very hot oven, the loaf springs up, then the yeast, having performed its function, is finally killed in the intense heat. Note that the only time that yeast is allowed to become hot is when the loaf is baked — the final stage of the whole process. In the earlier stages anything hotter than a warm atmosphere will prove disastrous. Yeast grows in warmth yet is killed at a high temperature. An airing cupboard provides the ideal temperature for yeast dough to rise. The equivalent may be to stand the dough near the kitchen boiler, or to put it near a fire or in a drying cabinet set at low.

Salt and the method by which it is introduced into the dough is important. If it is mixed with the yeast liquid or is in any way allowed to come into direct contact with the yeast, it will kill the yeast immediately. Salt, however, is vital to the flavour of bread: it must be measured accurately into the flour and then should be well incorporated before the yeast liquid is added. It does have some effect on the growth of yeast, however, but in slowing it down it also helps to form a good texture.

So far, remember that warmth and moisture and food in the form of flour make yeast grow but that extreme heat and direct salt will kill it.

Most people know of white flour, brown flour and self-raising flour. It is not until one starts breadmaking that yet another type becomes apparent, called strong or hard flour. The distinguishing protein within this strong flour is called gluten, which becomes elastic when the flour is mixed with a liquid to form a dough and subsequently kneaded. Kneading develops the gluten, making it stronger and able to stretch. A bread dough containing a large amount of gas after the yeast has fermented must be able to expand and support without breaking down. The structure thus formed becomes set during baking. Kneading should be rhythmic to give an even dough. The kneading pattern remains even after the bread is cooked and can be observed on a cut slice. It is especially apparent inside a French *baguette* as feathery circles when the bread is broken apart. A potentially good loaf, however, can be ruined by allowing the dough to go on rising for too long, causing overstretching and weakening of the structure. When this is allowed to happen, acids are formed, causing a sour flavour, the texture becomes close and the colour turns from white to grey. It is for these reasons that a dough must not be left to grow and grow during rising and proving — it has to be stopped.

The amount of liquid is vital. Great care should be taken not to get a tight dough in the beginning, for it is very difficult to make it soft and elastic afterwards. It is better to be on the safe side and make a slack dough in the beginning, adding more flour if necessary to make the consistency right. It is not always possible to get the same results each time even if you measure the ingredients accurately. Flours vary in quality, some absorbing more liquid than others and this has a bearing on results. A tight dough will produce a heavy loaf. A softer dough rises more quickly.

It is essential that the ingredients used in breadmaking are of top fresh quality because if stale flour or stale yeast is used, no matter how closely you follow the rules, you will not get a good result. This is discussed a little more fully later. Meanwhile we will look at a usual recipe and method for making a plain white loaf.

WHITE BREAD

450 g strong white flour; 2 level teaspoons salt; 15 to 25 g fresh yeast; 1 teaspoon sugar; 275 ml tepid water.

It will be observed that a fifth ingredient has been mentioned — sugar. Although this is not vital it does help to start the yeast working, acting as a food. It appears in most recipe books but is in no way meant to act as a sweetener. Have somewhere warm ready to put the dough to rise. If possible warm the flour and the mixing bowl before you start. The salt should be an accurate 2 teaspoons, obtained by scraping the excess salt from the teaspoon with a straight-edged knife.

The water should be measured into a jug and its temperature should be gauged by dipping the little finger into it. It should be the same as your body heat and feel like the same temperature. Proceed by measuring the flour and salt into a warm mixing bowl and mix well. Make a hollow in the middle. Put the yeast and sugar into a teacup or small basin and, using the back of a teaspoon, cream them together, pressing between the spoon and the inside of the cup. Within ½ a minute it will have turned liquid. Add a little of the measured tepid water and blend in. Pour all this yeast mixture back to the remaining water, scraping in any that is left in the cup. Now, remembering that we must not get a tight dough, you may remove one or two tablespoons of the flour from the bowl to a saucer and set aside. (This may or may not be required to achieve the right consistency later.) Add the yeast liquid to the flour *all at once* and using a wooden spoon incorporate all the flour with the liquid, bringing it in quickly from the sides of the bowl. If the dough is too slack to knead, start adding the reserved flour until you have a soft elastic dough that can be turned out on to a floured surface and kneaded by hand. Use only sufficient dusting flour to stop the dough from sticking. If too much flour is sprinkled on to the working surface it will become incorporated into the dough and make it dry and hard. Knead for a few minutes until the dough is smooth and even. Rinse out the mixing bowl and replace the dough. Cover the entire bowl with a plate or a damp tea towel and set in a warm place. The temperature should not exceed 30 °C (85 °F). Here it should remain until it has doubled in bulk. The warmer it is the faster it will rise. Also, if the dough contains the maximum amount of yeast it will rise more quickly than if the minimum amount is used. It is, however, better to use the minimum amount if time allows, since a better loaf is produced. It is also preferable to put dough to rise in a warm atmosphere rather than in a very warm one although, again, it will take longer. Rising takes 45 minutes or more.

It must be stressed that in any event the dough must be fully risen, meaning that the yeast has fully fermented. This is indicated by the dough having doubled in size and, if pressed with a finger, the indentation will remain and not spring back. If it is not fully risen the eventual loaf will be heavy and close in texture. If, on the other hand, it is left for too long, acids will be produced, causing a sour flavour, the structure will be weakened and the loaf will have a coarse, dark-coloured crumb. But having allowed it to rise nicely, scrape what will have become a very soft dough back on to the table and 'knock it back'. This term means to knead it a second time until most of the air bubbles have been squashed out. By cutting the dough in half, it is possible to ascertain how much air is left. If large holes are revealed these will expand in baking, causing a badly textured loaf. Kneading is done by pulling out the dough from the side with the right hand and pushing the end you are holding back into the bulk. The left hand gives an anticlockwise turn before the process is repeated. A rhythm will come eventually. If this evenly kneaded dough is turned upside down it should have a lovely smooth bottom, ideal as the top of a loaf of bread. So, without spoiling the shape, drop the dough into the bread tin: it should come half way up, and be domed. Should it not satisfy you after the first attempt, slip it back on the table, knead again, and reshape. (Note that the corners of the bread tin will be filled by the natural action of the dough during the proving process.) Brush the top of the dough with beaten egg to give a brown shiny crust when the loaf is baked.

This dough is again set in a warm place and allowed to rise until doubled, or until it has reached the top of the tin — this is known as proving. The whole tin of dough can be placed inside a loose polythene bag while it proves, which helps to prevent the crust drying out and becoming hard. However, it is a matter of choice. Meanwhile, put the oven on at regulo 8, 230 °C (450 °F) to preheat during the 10 minutes it will take the bread to prove. This proving is the last rising and, again, it is possible to underdo or to overdo it. When the dough is pressed with the finger it should now spring back — if an impression is left it is over-proved. By the time the loaf goes in the oven there should still be plenty of elasticity left for there to be a final rapid rising as the yeast works in the increased heat. This is called oven-spring and usually appears around the sides of the crust. It looks what it is, that is, stretched. On reaching a temperature of 50 °C (120 °F), the yeast is finally killed. After 10 minutes of being in the oven, the temperature is lowered to regulo 6, 200 °C (400 °F). The crust should have set, and the inside now needs to be cooked through. A large loaf will take approximately 1 hour altogether. Small loaves take about 35 minutes. When done, the loaf will sound hollow when turned out of its tin and the base knocked with the knuckles. It it is not cooked, or if the sides and bottom are not crisp and brown to your liking, simply return the loaf for a few more minutes to the oven, without its tin. To cool it is most important that this is done on a cooling rack, to allow steam to escape. If left in the tin, the steam will condense back into the loaf, making it 'sad', or heavy.

This all seems a lot to remember. There is only one thing to do: that is to get started. Put briefly, this is the order of things:

cream the yeast with water and allow to froth (*sponge*)
mix the dough
first *kneading*
rising in a warm place, covered
second *kneading* (*knocking back*)
shaping into a loaf
proving in warm place
baking

When making a larger amount of dough than in the given recipe, say three times as much flour, you do not use three times the yeast. Twice the amount is enough. However, suppose that you are making up the same amount of flour as in the recipe, 450 g, but time is short. It is possible to speed things up in two ways, as already suggested, that is, increase the rising temperature to maximum, approximately 30 °C (85 °F), and increase the amount of yeast from the minimum of 15 g to 25 g. More than 25 g is not acceptable.

When using dried yeast, the amounts and the preparation differ from what has been described. The amount to use is half the weight of fresh yeast. You would therefore use 15 g of dried in place of 30 g of fresh. Dried yeast takes more time to wake up and get working. You would proceed by dissolving the teaspoon of sugar in the measured tepid water and sprinkling the dried yeast lightly and evenly over the top. Then without stirring allow it to sink to the bottom, give it a brisk stir and stand it in a warm place to sponge. After 10 minutes there should be a frothy head on top of the water, showing that the yeast is both alive and ready to use. It has sponged. If, on the other hand, nothing happens after 10 minutes it is a sign that the yeast is stale (see p. 132). When dried yeast has sponged, continue as for fresh yeast. If it fails to sponge altogether do not go any further or you will only waste the flour: you must get some more live yeast, whether fresh or dried.

This chapter has described in general terms the behaviour of yeast and flour under the conditions for making bread. The reader will go on to make fruit breads, doughnuts, or any of the other rich mixtures, having the additional ingredients of sugar, fat, dried fruit and eggs. Although the underlying principles remain the same, one should note that these extra ingredients cause the yeast to work much more slowly. For this reason, a greater proportion of yeast is used, and a longer rising time is allowed. For buns having a lot of sugar, the cooking temperature, regulo 6, 200 °C (400 °F), is less than for bread at the outset. A higher temperature would make the outside burn before the inside was cooked.

BUYING AND STORING YEAST AND FLOUR

Fresh yeast is usually obtainable from a small bakers or a health food shop. It is beige in colour and if fresh will be moist and crumbly, having no brown marks on the outside showing that it is aging or that it has been left uncovered. Once bought, it should be kept in a cool place or in the refrigerator, wrapped in cling film or in foil to prevent drying. It will keep for several days in this way but become staler and less effective the longer it is kept. Use when as fresh as possible. The Flour Advisory Bureau carry out tests on yeast and will issue their findings via leaflets on request. They have tested yeast stored in the deep-freeze and maintain that no longer than 6 weeks is an advisable storage time. It is sometimes possible to keep it for longer than this, with luck. Dried yeast is obtainable from most food shops. It comes in sachets sufficient to make 1½ kg of flour into bread, or in vacuum-sealed tins of larger amounts. Most dried foods can be kept for well over a year without marked deterioration — some a lot longer. On the strength of this, yeast is often bought in the larger quantities by a new and enthusiastic breadmaker who sees the way to always being able to make a loaf or two whenever the urge or need arises, or should the fresh variety be unobtainable. When this eventually happens — perhaps a year later — the cook may suddenly assume that he or she has lost the touch when the bread fails to rise. But the cause is essentially stale yeast. Dried yeast, in fact, needs to be freshly dried yeast to be any good at all. It is safer to buy from an outlet with a large turnover — usually a supermarket — in order to be sure that it has not been sitting on the shelf for months on end. It is also safer to buy in small quantities, as and when one needs it. Dried yeast deteriorates faster once the vacuum seal is broken, another reason why it is preferable to buy in small quantities. Luckily, to avoid wasting the flour if one is not sure of the yeast, it is always possible to test the life in either kind before mixing the dough. One simply allows the yeast to sponge in the liquid with the sugar and, if nothing happens, throws it away and buys some more. If it shows no vigorous signs of life to begin with, it is unlikely to do anything later. The resulting loaf will be so heavy that the sparrows will refuse to eat it too.

Flour is another dried product that will not keep indefinitely. White flour keeps longer than brown and the Flour Advisory Bureau recommend 3 or 4 months for white, but only 4 to 6 weeks for wholemeal flour. Wholemeal and wheatmeal flours contain fat, which turns rancid. Old flour should be used up first and should on no account be mixed with a fresh lot. It should be stored dry and cool. Wholemeal flour does not contain the gluten found in a strong flour, so the method for making wholemeal bread is a little different, and can be found below.

Should one be unable to obtain strong flour at any time, it is usually possible to obtain from a health food shop a packet of gluten to mix with the soft flour. Follow the directions given to obtain the equivalent of a strong flour.

BROWN BREAD

This can be made with wholemeal flour or with a mixture of wholemeal and strong white flour. The proportions are up to you but, as a general guide, 80 per cent wholemeal and 20 per cent strong white make a satisfactory blend. 80 per cent wholemeal is called wheatmeal. Any brown loaf containing a proportion of white flour thus contains gluten, which provides a better structure and makes it less crumbly. Do not expect brown bread to have the same texture as white.

WHOLEMEAL BREAD

450 g wholemeal flour; 2 level teaspoons salt; 25 g fresh yeast; 1 teaspoon sugar; 275 ml tepid water.

Put the flour and salt into a large mixing bowl and mix well. Make a hollow in the middle. Cream the yeast and sugar in a small basin using a teaspoon. As it becomes liquid blend in the tepid water. Allow to sponge (ferment, indicated by a frothy head as on a glass of beer) for 20 minutes. Pour this ferment into the hollow all at once, then quickly mix with the flour, using a wooden spoon. As a dough is formed turn on to a floured board and knead for a few minutes or until the dough is evenly mixed. Miss out the rising stage as for white bread and proceed to shape the loaves. Divide the dough into two, knead each separately into a smooth-topped loaf and place in two 225 g loaf tins. Set in a warm place to prove until doubled in size. Meanwhile preheat the oven to regulo 8, 230 °C (450 °F). Bake the loaves for 10 minutes at regulo 8, 230 °C (450 °F), then reduce the temperature to regulo 6, 200 °C (400 °F) for the remainder of the cooking time — about 25 minutes, making 35 minutes in all.

Note There is no point in kneading wholemeal bread for longer than is required to mix it evenly because wholemeal flour does not contain the gluten that strong white flour has.

WHEATMEAL BREAD

Where a proportion of strong white flour is included in the flour mixture, proceed along the same lines as for plain white bread (see p. 128 for detailed instructions). The proportion is often 80 per cent wholemeal and 20 per cent strong white, but you can use equal quantities of both. It is purely a matter of taste.

Note I have found that wheatmeal bread made by the

traditional method of making white bread, as described, is more successful than wholemeal bread made according to the preceding recipe. The latter, however, is a recognised method.

HOT CROSS BUNS

Spiced rich yeast dough with dried fruit. Allow more time to make these than when making plain white bread dough because the additional fat and sugar slow down the process.

> *25 g fresh yeast; 1 teaspoon sugar; 250 ml milk; 450 g strong white flour; 2 level teaspoons salt; 25 g butter; 50 g sugar; 1 rounded teaspoon mixed spice; 100 g mixed dried fruit or currants; 1 egg; a little pastry to make crosses; Glaze: 100 ml milk; 3 table-spoons sugar.*

Cream the yeast and sugar in a basin. Warm the milk until tepid and add to the yeast mixture. In a large mixing bowl mix the flour and salt and rub in the butter. Add the sugar, spice and fruit and make a hollow in the centre. Beat the egg and add it together with the milk and yeast mixture to the flour. Use a wooden spoon to quickly incorporate the dry and liquid ingredients together so that they absorb evenly together. Turn on to a floured table and knead for a few minutes until smooth. Return the dough to the rinsed-out mixing bowl, cover with a plate and set to rise in a warm place until doubled in size. When risen, turn out on to a floured table and knead for 10 minutes. Divide the mixture into 12 pieces. Knead and shape each piece into a bun, placing side by side on a lightly greased metal baking sheet. Roll out the pastry for the crosses and cut 24 strips — each measuring 6 by ½ cm. Brush each bun with beaten egg and lay the crosses over. You can put the tray of buns inside a loose polythene bag or simply leave them open and set in a warm place to prove until doubled in size. Meanwhile preheat the oven to regulo 8, 230 °C (450 °F). Bake the buns for 15 to 20 minutes or until done. Make the glaze by simmering together the milk and sugar until it becomes thick and syrupy. Have the glaze ready to brush over the buns as soon as they come from the oven. When cool, remove the pastry crosses to reveal the same shape in white beneath.

14

Cakemaking

All cakes are made from the same four basic ingredients: fat, flour, eggs and sugar. The fifth element is the raising agent to make the cake light. This can be air or it can be a chemical that produces an expanding gas as the cake mixture heats up and bakes in the oven. (Self-raising flour already contains it—see p. 142.) These ingredients can be used in various proportions which affect the final texture and taste. It also means that a cake with, for example, a high proportion of fat is suitable for making by one method, and a cake not having any fat at all by another, and so on. It is according to the methods used that cakes are thus classified. These methods are rubbing in, creaming, melting and whisking. It is more useful to understand these four basic methods than simply to collect a large number of recipes. You will then be able to make a cake without looking at the instructions, and will know how to improvise and adapt.

These are the four methods.

RUBBING-IN METHOD

This is used for plain cakes. A plain cake is not necessarily one without fruit or spices but the term signifies a cake with a low proportion of fat to flour, containing less eggs than a rich cake. The proportion of fat is half or less than half fat to flour. You can therefore have a plain cherry cake or a plain fruit cake. The method is to cut the fat into small pieces and rub it into the flour with the fingertips until it resembles fine breadcrumbs. The sugar, egg and a small amount of liquid are then worked in with a wooden spoon, together with dried fruit if used. Plain cakes will not keep for very long. Because they contain little fat they quickly become dry, but can be stored for a few days in an airtight tin.

CREAMING METHOD

A cake is called a rich cake when there is upwards of half fat to flour. There are more eggs in a rich cake than in a plain one. The previous method (rubbing in) is quite unsuitable here, being too greasy to cope with by hand. Instead, the fat is creamed with the sugar using the back of a wooden spoon, until it becomes pale coloured, light and fluffy. The eggs are then beaten in and finally the flour is folded in, together with any fruit used. It is important to fold the flour in and not to beat it, otherwise it will make the cake tough. The sugar used is caster sugar, which is finer and dissolves more readily than granulated sugar. The flour used is self-raising flour, except in rich cakes containing a high proportion of fruit, such as a Christmas cake, when plain flour is used. Rich cakes keep for several weeks and some for months. They should be stored airtight.

WHISKING METHOD

A true sponge cake is made by the whisking method. Its lightness depends solely on the air whisked into it and not on a chemical raising agent as do all the others. For this reason plain flour should always be used for a sponge cake. The method is to whisk air into the eggs and sugar until they become pale, creamy, and voluminous, then carefully to fold in the flour. A true sponge contains no fat so therefore should be eaten on the day it is made, before it becomes dry. However, there is a variation called a Genoese sponge, where melted butter is folded into the mixture after the flour has been added. This is a moister cake and keeps for much longer. It is important in the making of this kind of cake that the eggs are not whisked too much. This distends the cell walls and causes the cake to collapse in the oven or when it comes out.

MELTING METHOD

Mixtures having a high proportion of sugar and treacle are made by this method. They are usually very dark and spicy, such as gingerbread. The treacle is melted with the butter and sugar, which is then poured into the spiced flour mixture also containing the raising agent. The raising agent in this type of cake is usually bicarbonate of soda because

(1) bicarbonate of soda helps to make the cake dark in colour, which is an advantage with gingerbreads and
(2) it acts more slowly in releasing the gas than baking powder used in conjunction with plain flour, and more slowly than self-raising flour used alone.

This type of cake is heavy because of the treacle used and a slower-acting raising agent is therefore more suitable. The flavour of the residue left in the cake after the reaction of the bicarbonate of soda (the residue is sodium carbonate) is masked by the spices and is not noticed when the cake is eaten. These cakes are baked at a low temperature.

The principles underlying cake making also apply to biscuits. The ingredients are the same except that the liquid is not added. Quite often a raising agent is not used. Cake mixtures may also become the basis of or form part of a pudding. Eve's pudding consists of fruit arranged in an ovenproof dish, covered with a rich cake mixture, which is then all baked until risen and golden. A steamed treacle pudding is also made from a rich cake mixture. A fruit crumble has a topping made by the rubbing-in method.

If you analyse a selection of cake recipes in any cookery book you will conclude that a Christmas cake is made by the creaming method, while a Christmas yule log is made by the whisking method, raspberry buns by the rubbing-in method and brandysnaps and gingerbread are both examples of a biscuit and a cake made by the melting method.

The interrelation of the ingredients and how they are affected by the cook and by the oven temperature are complicated. Although it is quite possible to make cakes successfully without a full understanding, you will be more consistently successful if you know what is going on. Notes on the cooking of eggs should be read (see p. 8), as also should chapters 12 and 13 on pastrymaking and breadmaking, since both are concerned with the use of flour.

INGREDIENTS USED IN CAKEMAKING

It is essential to follow the recipe since the form and amount of each ingredient affect the behaviour of the others. The oven temperature is vital as also is the size of the tin.

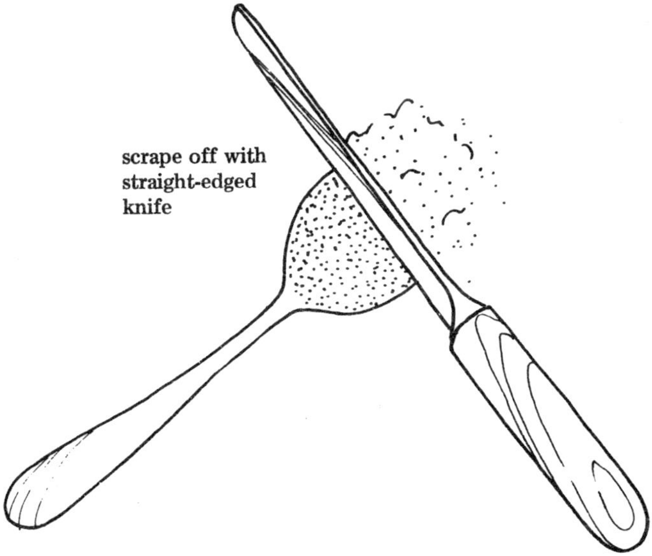

Figure 14.1 A level spoon

Figure 14.2 A rounded spoon

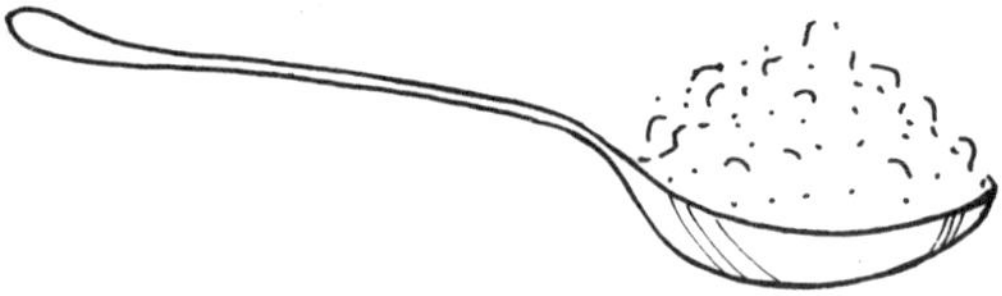

Figure 14.3 A heaped spoon

Recipes frequently tell you to use a level spoon, a rounded spoon or a heaped spoon of some ingredient. When measuring a level spoon (figure 14.1) you should scrape off the excess with a straight-edged knife. A rounded spoon means that there is as much above the bowl of the spoon as there is in it (figure 14.2). A heaped spoon means that there is about twice as much above the bowl of the spoon as there is in it (figure 14.3).

Flour

For cakemaking, soft flour (also called weak flour) should be used. This contains less gluten than hard or strong flour. Strong flour contains 16 per cent gluten, all-purpose flour contains 10.5 per cent, while cake flour has 7.5 per cent. A flour can be made soft by replacing some of it with cornflour. When flour is manipulated with water or another liquid the gluten becomes elastic and when baked this becomes semi-rigid. This is essential to a certain degree to produce a structure. If a cake mixture is beaten, however, it will become tough because the gluten in flour is developed by being beaten. Gluten development is also affected by the ratio of fat to sugar to liquid. Fat acts as a control since it coats the gluten strands so that they slide by each other and are not able to form a tacky substance and become elastic. It is only for baked goods which undergo great structural stress as in breadmaking and in the making of strudel dough that strong flour is needed so that it does not rupture. In a dry mix the gluten will not develop as quickly as in a fluid one. Sugar and the cold also delay gluten development. This is one of the reasons that everything is kept cold in pastry-making.

Eggs

The value of these in cakemaking is due to a combination of factors. Eggs are partly responsible for making cakes light, while in a sponge they are totally responsible. They have the ability to entrap air whisked into them to produce a foam. This light foam is then made to support the addition of flour, which is folded in, and the mixture is then baked. The air expands and the cake rises even more. They also act as a solvent, they add colour, flavour and help to bind the mixture together.

Fats (Shortenings)

These help to make cakes tender. The fat coats the gluten strands in the flour so that they slide by one another and the cake mixture does not therefore become tough very easily. Some fats are better than others—soft fats are excellent, as are those with free fatty acids. Butter, margarine, lard, clean dripping and oil can all be used in cakemaking. In strongly flavoured cakes, for example, gingerbreads, it is a good idea to use lard rather than butter because butter is more expensive and we would not be able to appreciate its flavour when hidden by spices. For cakes not having any additional flavourings it is a good idea on the other hand to use butter. Butter also gives colour to a cake.

Liquids

Eggs contain 75 per cent water and are thus considered as

one of the liquids in a cake. Essences may be dissolved in the liquid and are therefore readily dispersed throughout. It is especially important for the raising agent, which will not work until dissolved. Liquid is also necessary for the starch in the flour to gelatinise; it absorbs it, thus making the cake moist.

Raising Agents

These may be natural, such as air, steam and yeast. Most cakes rely for their lightness to a certain degree on air and steam but to a greater degree on the result of a chemical raising agent which produces carbon dioxide within the raw cake mixture. This gas is produced when the chemicals are first mixed with a liquid and then heated. For this reason, a cake should be baked as soon as it is mixed, otherwise the chemicals will have worked and their effectiveness lost. Baking powder (used in conjunction with plain flour) contains bicarbonate of soda and cream of tartar. It also contains a substance which keeps the mixture dry. Self-raising flour already contains these substances and is convenient to use in cakes. Bicarbonate of soda is used alone for gingerbreads.

Sugar

Sweetening a cake is not the only reason why sugar is used in cakemaking. It increases the volume of a mixture when creamed with fat since it helps to entrap air. It also raises the final coagulation temperature of the gluten within the flour so that the cake has more time to expand. Sugar is also responsible for the colour, and to some extent the actual flavour of a cake, in that it turns to caramel on the outside, making it brown.

PLAIN RAISIN AND WALNUT CAKE

A plain cake used in this context means one not having a

large proportion of fat to flour as does a rich cake.

225 g self-raising flour; 75 g butter; 75 g granulated sugar; 125 g raisins; 1 egg; 150 ml milk; 50 g walnuts.

Grease and line with greased greaseproof paper a 17 cm cake tin. Preheat the oven to regulo 5, 190 °C (375 °F). Sieve the flour into a bowl. Cut up the fat and add it to the flour. Rub together with the fingertips until the mixture resembles fine breadcrumbs. It should still be light in colour and not have become dark yellow and oily. Stir in the sugar and the raisins. Beat the egg and milk together. Make a hollow in the flour, add the liquid all at once then use a wooden spoon to quickly incorporate and form a soft dough. Do not beat it. Turn the mixture into the prepared tin. Chop the walnuts and scatter over the smoothed surface of the cake mixture. Bake for the first 15 minutes at regulo 5, 190 °C (375 °F), then lower to regulo 4, 180 °C (350 °F) for a further 45 minutes or until firm. The cake should remain positioned in the centre of the oven. Remove from the tin and cool on a wire rack.

To line the cake tin you need a length of greaseproof paper

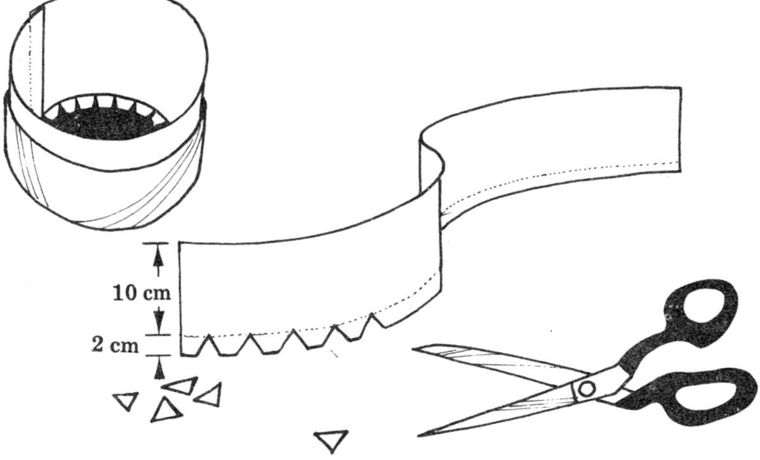

Figure 14.4 Lining a cake tin

which is as long as the circumference of the tin and at least as tall. Make a crease right down the edge of the paper about 2 cm wide. Flatten it out so that you can use a pair of scissors to nick small triangles, as shown in figure 14.4. Grease the inside of the cake tin and position the paper (the greasy surface holds the paper in place). Cut a circle of greaseproof paper to fit and cover the base of the tin. Finally brush the entire surface of the greaseproof paper with more melted lard or butter after which it is ready to be filled with the cake mixture and cooked.

Note This is an example of a cake made by the rubbing-in method. These are made light chiefly by the addition of a chemical raising agent, either by using self-raising flour, or a combination of plain flour and baking powder. The same mixture can be baked as small buns but needs to be baked at a higher temperature than for a cake, at regulo 6, 200 °C (400 °F). When done, cakes and buns should be slightly shrunk away from the sides of the tin and there should be no hissing.

VICTORIA SANDWICH

A cake having recognised proportions of fat, flour, sugar and eggs. Since there are no fruits or spices in a Victoria sandwich it is preferable to use butter for the flavour it gives.

125 g self-raising flour; 125 g butter; 125 g caster sugar; 2 large eggs; Filling: 1 to 2 tablespoons red jam; To finish: icing sugar.

Preheat the oven to regulo 5, 190 °C (375 °F). Grease the inside of two 17 cm sandwich tins with melted butter. Toss in a spoonful of flour, roll around to coat evenly, then tap out the excess. Proceed with the cake mixture by measuring the flour on to a plate. In a large mixing bowl cream together the butter and sugar until soft, light and fluffy. (It helps if the bowl is warm and the eggs and butter are at room temperature.) Use a wooden spoon, beating the butter against the inside of the bowl. Scrape the mixture to one side and break one egg into the space that remains. Add a teaspoon of the measured flour and beat until the egg is broken up, ignoring the butter and sugar at first but then gradually incorporating it in. Repeat this process with the second egg, remembering to incorporate the mixture very slowly to prevent curdling. Every so often use a plastic spatula to scrape the mixture off the spoon and from the inside of the bowl, and mix in with the rest. Add the remaining flour and fold it in with the spatula until you have a soft-dropping consistency. It is important not to beat the flour into the mixture but to gently fold it in, otherwise it will make the cake tough. Divide the mixture between the two sandwich tins and smooth over the top. Bake in the middle of the oven for about 20 minutes or until well risen, golden and firm to the touch. Turn on to a cooling rack. When cold, spread one cake with the softened jam and place the other on top. Dust with icing sugar through a tea-strainer. (This is finer than an ordinary sieve.)

Note This is an example of a cake made by the creaming method. The sugar used should always be caster sugar, which blends more quickly with the butter to produce a light fluffy cream. Vanilla or other essence if used should be beaten with the eggs. Cocoa used to make a chocolate Victoria sandwich cake should be sifted with the flour; the cocoa replaces some of the flour and is not used in addition to it.

RICH FRUIT CAKE

This is based on a Victoria sandwich.

225 g self-raising flour; ¼ teaspoon mixed spice; 225 g butter; 225 g caster sugar; 4 large eggs; 125 g glacé cherries; 450 g mixed dried fruit; 125 g walnuts.

Grease and line with greased greaseproof paper a 20 cm cake tin. Preheat the oven to regulo 2, 150 °C (300 °F). Measure the flour and spice on to a plate. In a large mixing bowl cream together the butter and sugar until soft, light and fluffy, using a wooden spoon. Scrape the mixture to one side and break one egg into the space that remains. Add a teaspoon of the measured flour and beat with the egg until it is broken up, ignoring the butter and sugar at first but then gradually incorporating it in. Repeat this process with the second egg, then with the third and fourth separately, remembering to incorporate the mixture very slowly to prevent curdling. Every so often use a plastic spatula to scrape the mixture off the spoon and from the inside of the bowl and mix it in with the rest. Cut the cherries in half and add these together with the flour and fruit to the mixture, folding them in until it becomes a soft-dropping consistency. Turn the mixture into the prepared tin and smooth over the top. Chop the walnuts and scatter on to the surface. Bake in the middle of the oven for 4 hours. Remove from the tin and allow to cool on a wire rack.

SPONGE CAKE

A very light cake relying solely on air for its lightness. A true sponge contains no fat.

125 g caster sugar; 4 large eggs; 125 g plain flour; Filling: 1 to 2 tablespoons red jam; 200 ml double cream, whipped; To finish: icing sugar.

Stand a large mixing bowl on a saucepan containing a few cups of water. Bring to the boil, then remove from the heat. Meanwhile grease and flour two 20 cm sandwich tins. Do this by brushing the inside with melted butter, adding a little flour and rolling the flour around the tin until it is all coated. The excess should be tapped out. Preheat the oven to regulo 5, 190 °C (375 °F). Proceed with the sponge by putting the sugar into the hot bowl while it still stands over the pan of water. Break the eggs into the sugar not allowing them to touch the hot bowl. Use a rotary whisk to beat the sugar and eggs to a light foam, 'to the ribbon', which means that when the beater is held above the mixture a thick trail of the mixture falls back into the bowl. This whisking should be done immediately and quickly. If left, the eggs will start to cook on the inside of the bowl. Remove the bowl from the pan and continue whisking the mixture until cool. Sift the flour lightly and evenly over the surface, folding it into the mixture as you do so. On no account must the mixture be beaten, otherwise it will collapse into a close tacky mass. Divide the mixture between the prepared tins and bake in the middle of the oven for 20 minutes or until it is slightly shrunk and springs back when pressed. Allow to cool for 2 minutes, then remove to a cooling rack. When cold you can fill with jam and whipped cream. Dust with icing sugar sprinkled through a tea-strainer.

Note This is an example of a cake made by the whisking method. Plain flour is always used for this type of cake, its lightness depending on air incorporated via the addition of whisked egg whites. Some of the flour can be replaced by cornflour to produce a soft flour which will make the cake softer and more tender. This mixture is the same as for Swiss rolls. It is not a suitable base to which to add fruit since the fruit would be too heavy and would sink. Liquid flavourings must be concentrated, while cocoa used for a chocolate cake replaces some of the flour. Coffee powder can also be used as a flavouring and should be blended with a small amount of boiling water to dissolve the coffee first before being folded into the mixture before the flour.

GENOESE SPONGE

This is based on a true sponge, with the addition of melted butter. It is moist and keeps well.

The ingredients are as for sponge cake on p. 146, with the addition of 50 g melted butter. Prepare the sponge in exactly the same way, then carefully fold in the melted butter at the end. Bake in the same way.

GINGERBREAD

Bicarbonate of soda is the chemical raising agent used in this type of cake, giving off carbon dioxide which expands in the oven to make the cake light. The residue (sodium carbonate) resulting from the chemical reaction of the raising agent is masked by the colour and flavour of the spices and black treacle.

175 g plain flour; 1 level teaspoon bicarbonate of soda; 1 level dessertspoon ground ginger; 1 rounded teaspoon cinnamon; 125 g lard; 125 g black treacle; 125 g brown sugar; 150 ml milk; 1 egg.

Grease and line with greased greaseproof paper a gingerbread tin 20 cm square. Preheat the oven to regulo 2, 150 °C (300 °F). Sift the flour, bicarbonate of soda, ginger and cinnamon into a large mixing bowl. Melt the lard slowly in a saucepan. Stand the saucepan on the scales and spoon the treacle into it until you have the right amount indicated. Add the sugar. Warm this mixture and stir until all is melted. The mixture must not be hot, however. Make a hollow in the flour and pour the mixture in. Stir until well blended. Do not beat it. Rinse the saucepan with the milk if necessary then add to the mixture with the beaten egg. Stir in. Pour into the prepared tin. Bake in the middle of the oven for 2 hours.

Note This is an example of a cake made by the melting method. You will find that this method varies slightly from book to book. The fat used can be lard, margarine, butter or clear dripping, but butter is a waste of money in this recipe because its flavour would be masked by the spice. Dark sugar is always used for gingerbreads. Gingerbread should be stored for a few days wrapped in foil, after which it will become sticky.

15

A Pie-crust, a Flan-case and a Vol-au-vent

PIE

A pie-dish has a rim on which to anchor the pie-crust (figure 15.1*a*). Properly done, the pastry cannot then shrink away from the sides and fall on top of the filling. Pies made in straight-sided Pyrex or soufflé dishes, or indeed anything else without the all-important rim, are far more difficult and are more likely to be unsuccessful. Sometimes the pie-filling fails to fill the dish, leaving a gap between itself and the crust. In this case, or when the filling is a very moist one, a pie-funnel should be used to support the pastry in the middle. This also allows steam to escape so that the pastry bakes better. An alternative method of supporting the crust of a large pie is to use four thin sticks laid criss-cross over the top of the dish which can then be withdrawn when the pie is cooked.

The choice of pastry for a pie is entirely personal, although puff pastry, rough puff and flaky are best suited to savoury pies, while shortcrust is suitable for both sweet and savoury ones. Allow 50 or more grams of flour per person, for

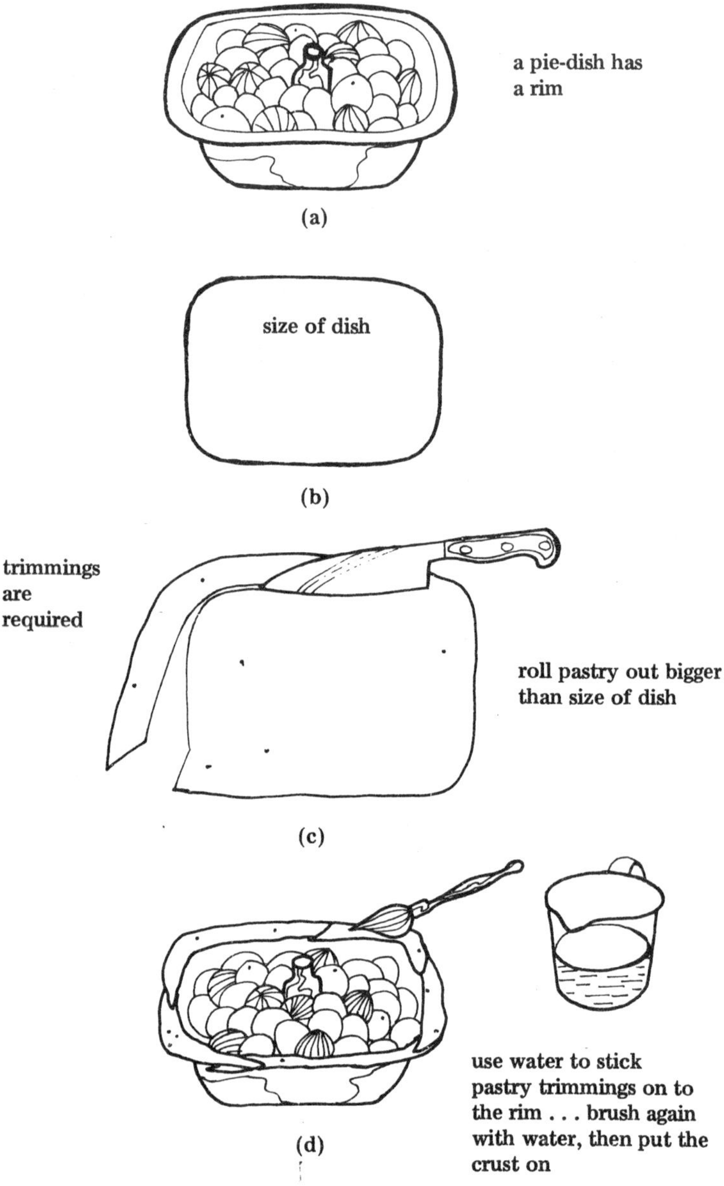
a pie-dish has a rim
(a)
size of dish
(b)
trimmings are required
roll pastry out bigger than size of dish
(c)
use water to stick pastry trimmings on to the rim . . . brush again with water, then put the crust on
(d)

Figure 15.1 How to make a pie-crust

example, for four persons, the pie-crust should be made with 225 g of flour.

Having chosen the type and then made the pastry, proceed to make the crust by rolling it out to about 4 cm bigger all round than the dish itself and of the same shape, square, round or oval (figure 15.1*b* and *c*). Cut out the crust itself slightly larger than the diameter of the dish to allow for any shrinkage. In addition to the crust you should now have trimmings of pastry — strips about 3 cm wide. Decide whether a pie-funnel is needed and place it in position. Moisten the rim of the pie-dish with water and firmly press the pastry strips on to it. It will look untidy at this stage but that does not matter (figure 15.1*d*). Now moisten the pastry rim with water, ready to take the crust. Lift the pastry from the table on to the rolling pin, then lift the rolling pin with the pastry dangling over it to the pie dish. Gently, now, press the crust on to the pastry rim. Take care not to press so hard as to pinch it and make it thin and uneven. Now hold the pie in your left hand while using a sharp knife in your right to slice off any surplus, slicing away from you.

These trimmings can be re-rolled and made into leaves and tassels for decoration. Roll out a length of pastry measuring 4 by 20 cm (figure 15.2). Use a sharp knife to cut the pastry as shown, then roll up around the thumb to form a tassel. The tassel should be fixed in position around the protruding pie-funnel if one is being used, using a little water to stick it firmly. A pastry tassel fixed on a raised pie can be placed in the centre, although there will be no pie-funnel on this kind of pie (see veal and ham pie, p. 42).

Use the fingertips to flute the edge of the pie (figure 15.3). Make two or three snips on top with scissors to allow steam to escape. If a funnel is used, simply allow it to poke through a hole in the top. The reason for this double thickness of pastry around the edge is that whereas most of the crust has a moist filling beneath, the rim tends to dry out more quickly and thus to burn. By doing it in the correct way as described, the pie both looks and cooks better.

In the Far East, the method used to hold up a pastry crust on a pie is to lay bamboo sticks crossways over the dish which are later removed when the pie is served (figure 15.4). To do this, follow the directions above on how to make a pie-crust but, before putting the crust over, lay the sticks over the rim of the dish on top of the pastry trimmings.

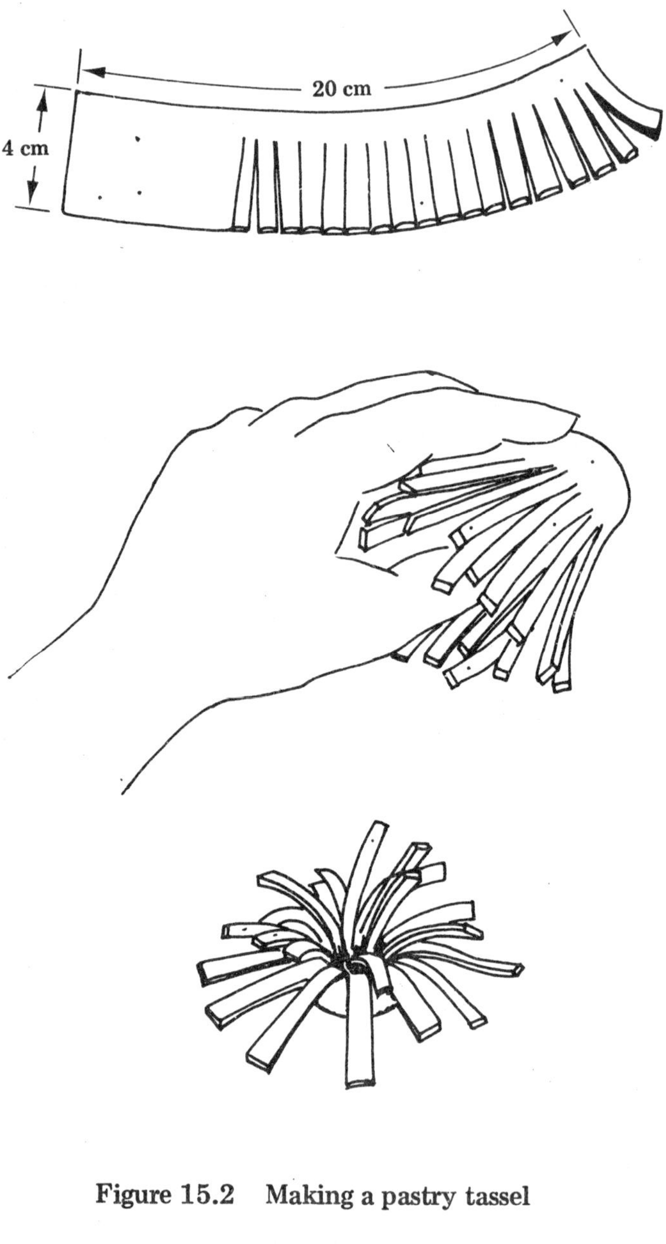

Figure 15.2 Making a pastry tassel

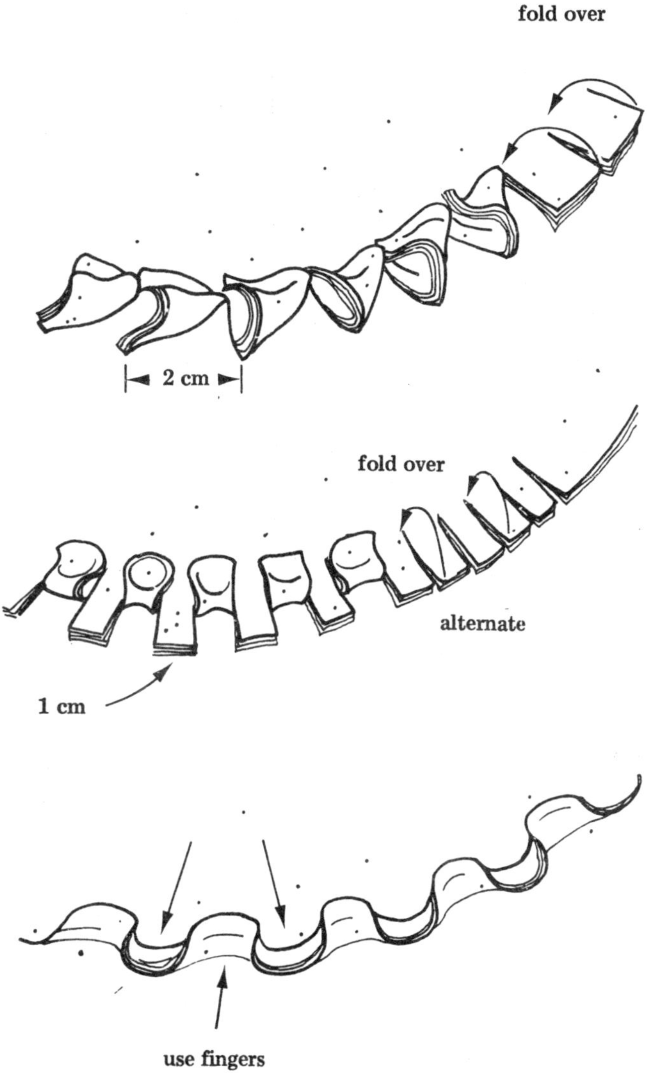

Figure 15.3 Fluting the edges of the pie

Figure 15.4 Another way of holding up a pie-crust

If the pie is a savoury one, brush the pastry with egg before baking it, to make it brown and shiny. If sweet, sprinkle with caster sugar either before or after baking.

As a general rule, shortcrust pies are baked in a preheated regulo 5, 190 °C (375 °F) oven while puff and flaky pastry must go into a very hot oven, regulo 8, 230 °C (450 °F), then lowered to regulo 6, 200 °C (400 °F) after the first 10 minutes. The time ultimately depends on what the filling is and whether it is to be baked from raw or has been cooked previously. You should cook the pie according to your recipe.

FLAN CASE (BAKED BLIND)

A ceramic flan dish, a metal flan tin or a simple metal flan hoop laid on a baking sheet can be used to make a pastry flan case. I prefer a metal flan tin with a removable base. Metal conducts heat better than ceramic, therefore the pastry cooks better. Many people prefer to cook and serve flans in the fluted dishes, however, because they look attractive on the table.

Some recipes call for a flan case 'baked blind', that is, baked empty. The raw filling is then put into the case and this goes back into the oven a second time to cook the filling itself. Making an empty flan case is where many people fail, because when it comes from the oven, what was a pastry case with sides to it often comes out as a flat pancake. Another general problem is concerned with the crispness of the pastry beneath the filling. This second problem is difficult to overcome—almost impossible using our ordinary domestic ovens. It is a fact that the French, famous for all kinds of delicious tarts, sweet and savoury, use ovens specially suited to this purpose. The French gas ovens are heated from beneath so that the 'floor' of one of these becomes burning hot. An uncooked flan is placed on the floor, which quickly cooks the pastry through and also browns it. The filling is then added and the flan is placed in the middle of the oven to cook the filling at a more gentle rate. You will already realise that an English oven is quite cool at the bottom, and is not well suited to baking flan cases in the same way as the French ones.

The pastry to use is shortcrust, rich shortcrust (often referred to in cookery books as flan pastry) or *pâte brisée*. There again, the French have a pastry which is perfect for flans, being not so short and crumbly in texture as shortcrust. *Pâte brisée* is flakier and rather more firm and will support the filling without breaking. It takes longer to make and then requires resting before use.

Whatever pastry you choose to use, proceed to roll it out thinly to about ¼ cm thick in a circle about 4 cm bigger all round than the flan tin itself. Lift the pastry on to the rolling pin (figure 15.5*a*), then holding the end of the rolling pin take the pastry to the flan tin and loosely drape it over. Lift the edge of the pastry, easing the slack into the corners. Do not stretch it or poke at it because this would cause shrinkage. Use a pastry brush dipped in water to moisten the inside rim of the flan. This sounds strange, but its purpose is to hold the uncooked pastry to it while it cooks so that it does not shrink away and become a flat pancake instead (figure 15.5*b*). Make a pleat as shown (figure 15.5*c*). Trim off the surplus pastry using a knife or simply roll the rolling pin over it, which cuts it off. Now flour the back of your first finger of your right hand and push against the inside rim, using the surplus pleat to raise the edge a little above the metal rim (figure 15.5*d*). Make the edge slightly rounded; if you pinch it thin it looks untidy and will burn quickly. If the flan tin has a fluted edge, press the finger into each little indentation. Be reasonably firm about pressing the pastry

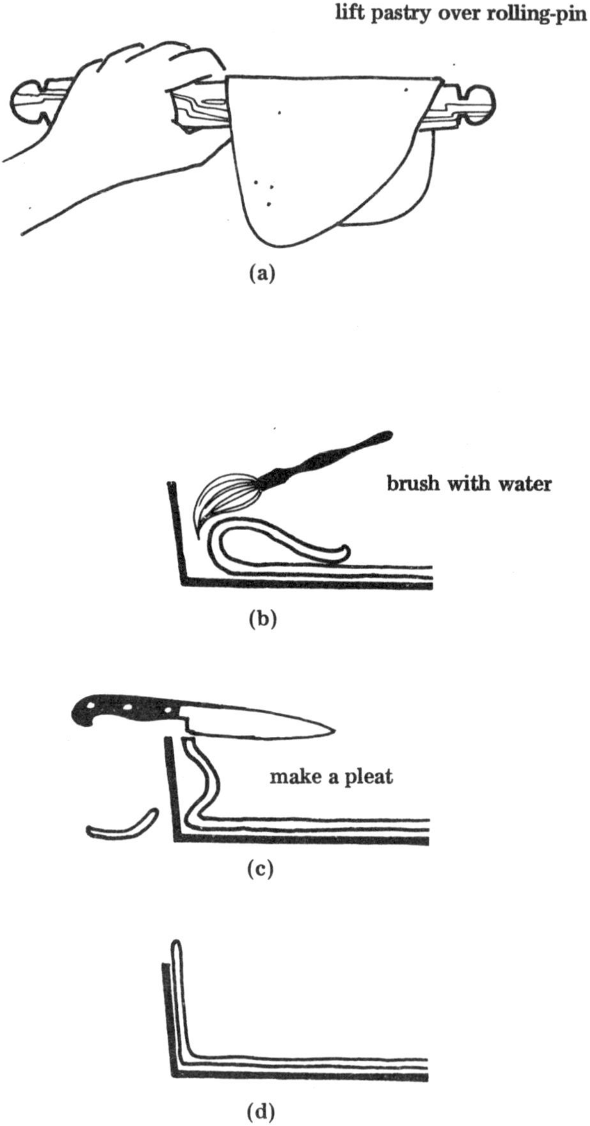

Figure 15.5 How to make a flan case

well on to the tin so that it holds well. Remember, we do not want it to shrink away. Before baking, use a fork to prick the bottom. The flan should go into a preheated oven, regulo 5, 190 °C (375 °F) on the middle shelf. If it goes on the top shelf, the edges will burn quickly. Look at it after 2 or 3 minutes, and if it has started to rise in the middle as it might, prick it once more in the middle and as the air escapes it will go down. Some recipe books will ask you to prevent this happening by placing a sheet of greaseproof paper in the flan with baking beans on it to hold the pastry down. This method, however, tends not to allow the pastry to cook so nicely. It will take about 10 minutes to cook, and should be firm and starting to turn a pale gold. The edges should be just beginning to colour: remember, the flan has to go back into the oven a second time to bake with its filling, so the edges must not be too brown the first time.

When done, remove from the oven and use as in the recipe.

A VOL-AU-VENT

Use either bought or home-made puff pastry for this. It is easier and less wasteful to make a rectangular vol-au-vent. Roll the pastry out to the thickness of a pencil, keeping a rectangular shape. For some people this is not so easy! When they put a rolling pin to it, it goes out of shape. The best way to get it right is first to depress the pastry with the rolling pin at intervals all along it—do not start to roll it out yet. This will make it slightly bigger. Turn it through 90° and repeat. Using even pressure on both ends of the rolling pin, roll the pastry in one direction. At this stage many people automatically press harder on their right side without knowing it, so that the pastry goes out farther on the right side. Roll it to an even thickness from the top to the bottom edge, turn the pastry through 90°, and do the same again. If your pastry now looks like the sketch (figure 15.6*a*) it is because when you rolled it the first time it looked like figure 15.6*b*, that is, you failed to make it of even thickness; the top and bottom edges being thicker automatically bulge out.

Having rolled the pastry to the thickness of a pencil in a neat rectangle, cut a frame from it (figure 15.7*a*). Carefully

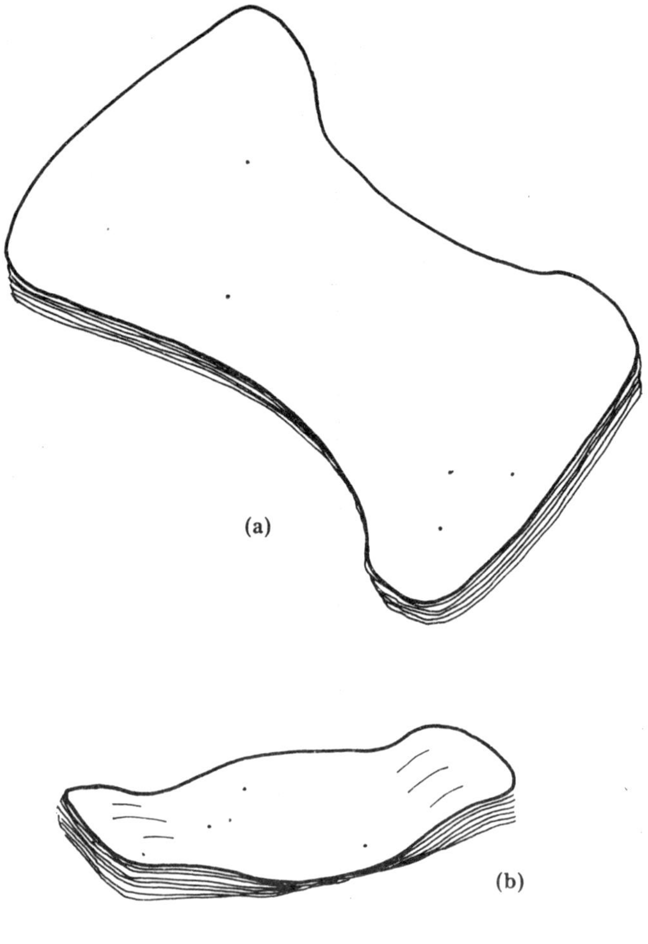

Figure 15.6 How *not* to roll pastry out

put the frame to one side (figure 15.7*b*). Place the rectangle in front of you, and roll this out until its outside dimension is the same as the frame (figure 15.7*c* and *d*). It is of course now much thinner than the frame and that is what we want. Lay the rectangle on a baking sheet, and moisten the edge with a little water. Do not flood it but use the minimum amount. Lift the pastry frame over the rolling pin and take

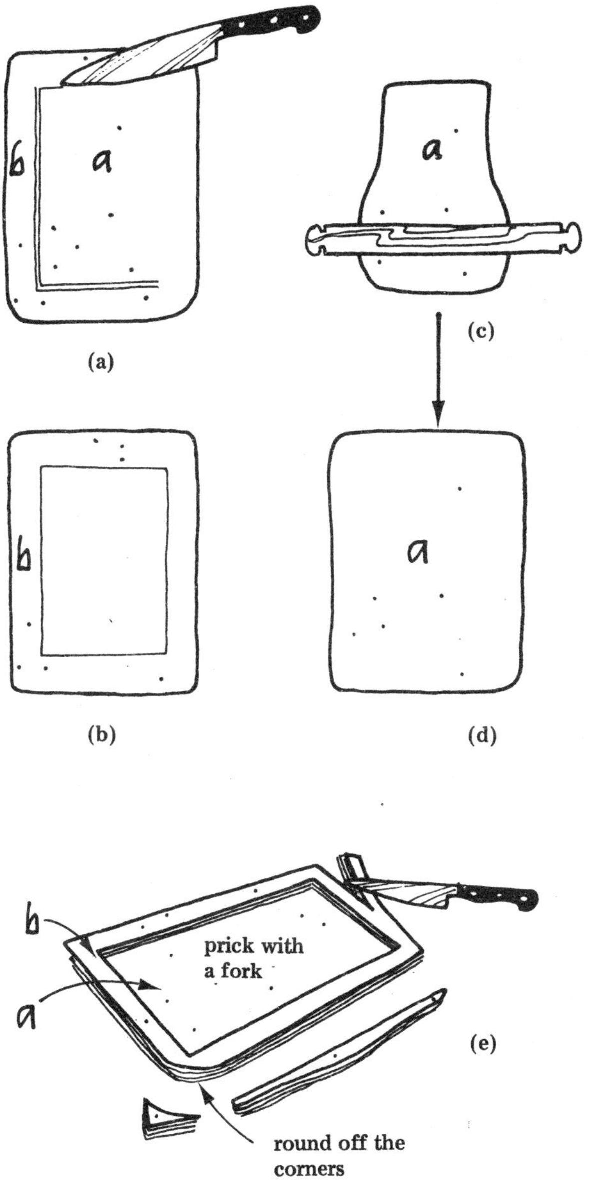

Figure 15.7 How to make a vol-au-vent case

it to the baking sheet. Ease it to fit on top of the rectangle. Use a long sharp dry knife dipped in a little flour to trim away the edges, making a firm decisive cut to do this rather than dragging the point of the knife through. Round off the corners, which will burn if you leave them on. Prick the base of the vol-au-vent with a fork to stop it rising (figure 15.7*e*). The vol-au-vent can be brushed with beaten egg to glaze but, be careful, since any egg that dribbles over the very edge of the pastry down its side will form a hard seal as soon as it goes into the hot oven, so preventing the layers from separating and rising up into a light, airy flakiness. Nor must you handle the cut edges of puff pastry or pinch it together in any way since this will also prevent it from rising, thus spoiling the finished result. Be careful in the way you actually cut the pastry because if the point of the knife is dragged through it will tend to seal it together. Puff pastry should be cut very decisively with a sharp and dry knife.

Place the vol-au-vent in the middle to top of a preheated hot oven, regulo 8, 230 °C (450 °F). This is the temperature for any item made with puff pastry. It should remain at this temperature for 10 minutes, after which the heat should be lowered to regulo 6, 200 °C (400 °F) for a further 20 minutes, making 30 minutes in all. Remember that ovens vary so much and use your judgement.

A vol-au-vent can be served hot with a savoury filling. In this case, it is best to heat the filling separately from the pastry case and to fill just before serving. If you heat the two together in the oven, it will make the pastry soggy. When reheating pastry do it in a slow oven, regulo 3 to 4, 170 to 180 °C (325 to 350 °F), not at the high temperature at which it originally cooked, otherwise it will burn. A vol-au-vent can also be filled cold with confectioner's custard and fruit arranged on top, and glazed with sieved apricot jam.

16

Cheesecakes

Farmers' wives in all stock-rearing countries have made cheeses and cheesecakes to use up excess milk — in the United Kingdom, France, Italy, Germany, the United States, and so on. From practical and humble beginnings cheesecakes have more recently become popular and fashionable in homes and nearly always feature on sweet trolleys in restaurants. They have been developed from the original knobbly curd tart dotted with currants to light foam concoctions and to rich, heavy creamy creations topped with bilberries, cherries, blackcurrants or some other sharp fruit to counteract the richness. There are many cheesecake *aficionados*.

Basically there are two kinds of cheesecake. There is one made of cheese set with eggs baked in the oven while the other is a light egg-foam type which is a cheesecake set with gelatine and is not cooked at all. Either kind can be made with cottage cheese, curd cheese or cream cheese. All of these are fresh (unfermented) cheeses. The main difference between them is in the amount of fat present. Cream cheese contains a lot of fat and is therefore very rich while cottage cheese contains hardly any. Curd cheese comes somewhere between the two. A rich cheese is made from milk with extra cream added, a less rich one with whole milk on its own, while cottage cheese is made from skimmed milk.

In other countries the equivalent fresh cheeses of course have other names: there is Italian *Ricotta* or Italian *Mozzarella* and there is French *Petit Suisse*. These are the varieties used to make cheesecakes in those countries. There may be other differences in the continental cheeses, however, for example, Italian *Ricotta* is made from ewe's milk, not cow's milk, and it is made *un*usually from the whey of the milk. Most are made from the curds. Buffalo's and goat's milk are also used.

Cheesecakes can be the simplest of curd tarts, baked in an open pastry crust on a shallow plate or in a flan tin. The basic ingredients of the traditional cooked cheesecake are fresh cheese, a little sugar, butter and eggs. Proportions vary according to taste, as they should. It is usual to introduce some other flavouring as well: grated lemon rind with nutmeg and currants is a popular combination. Ground almonds are sometimes added, or vanilla essence, or orange flower water.

More often, cheesecakes are made deeper in a loose-bottomed cake tin to be unmoulded when set or when cooled. A base is made of crushed digestive biscuits, Nice or ginger biscuits, often spiced, blended with butter and packed into the bottom of the tin before the filling is poured in. An alternative to biscuit crumbs is a thin layer of sponge cake which is lighter and possibly more suitable for the foam type of cheesecakes. A very rich cheesecake when cooked, or set, is often topped with fresh fruit or with sharp blackcurrants, the juice of which is sweetened, then thickened with a little cornflour. An unadorned cheesecake, however, can be accompanied by a few fresh grapes, which help to clear the palate.

The recipes that follow are for three very different cheese-cakes, a simple Yorkshire curd tart made in pastry, a very rich vanilla-flavoured one with a crumb base and a light lemon-flavoured foam type.

YORKSHIRE CURD TART

A homely style of cheesecake, flavoured with lemon and nutmeg, baked in a pastry case.

125 g shortcrust pastry (see p. 115); 125 g butter; 100 g caster sugar; 250 g cottage cheese; 2 eggs; 125 g currants; grated rind ½ lemon; nutmeg; a handful white breadcrumbs.

Line a 20 cm flan tin with the pastry (as described on p.156). Preheat the oven to regulo 5, 190 °C (375 °F). Cream together the butter and sugar in a large bowl using a wooden spoon until soft. Beat in the cheese, then the eggs and currants. Grate the lemon rind and the nutmeg on the fine edge of the grater and add these to your taste. The mixture will now be fairly fluid. Stir in a handful or so of breadcrumbs to firm it a little and to absorb some of the moisture. Turn this mixture into the prepared pastry case. Bake in the middle of the oven for 40 minutes, or until the mixture has set. Serve warm.

LEMON CHEESECAKE

An uncooked foam type of cheesecake with a light sponge base.

> *10 g powdered gelatine; 2 to 3 tablespoons cold water; 250 g curd cheese; 100 g caster sugar, 2 eggs, 175 ml double cream; 50 g sultanas; juice and grated rind 1 lemon; a 20 cm circle sponge cake, ½ cm thick.*

Sprinkle the gelatine on to the surface of the cold water in a very small saucepan. Without using a spoon to stir, gently swish the pan over the heat until the water just comes up to the boil and the gelatine is dissolved. It will look foamy at first but after you have set it aside for a few seconds to cool it will become clear. Beat together the cheese and sugar in a large bowl, using a wooden spoon. Separate the eggs. Put the whites into a clean basin. Add the yolks to the cheese, together with the cream, the sultanas and the lemon juice and rind. Mix evenly. Stir in the cool but still melted gelatine. (If the gelatine has started to set in the pan, warm it for a few seconds over the heat to remelt it.) Whisk the whites until stiff then carefully fold in to the mixture. Lay the circle of sponge in the bottom of a loose-bottomed 20 cm cake tin. Pour the mixture on to it, smoothing over the top. Allow to set for several hours in a cool place or in the refrigerator. Remove it from the tin as shown on p. 165.

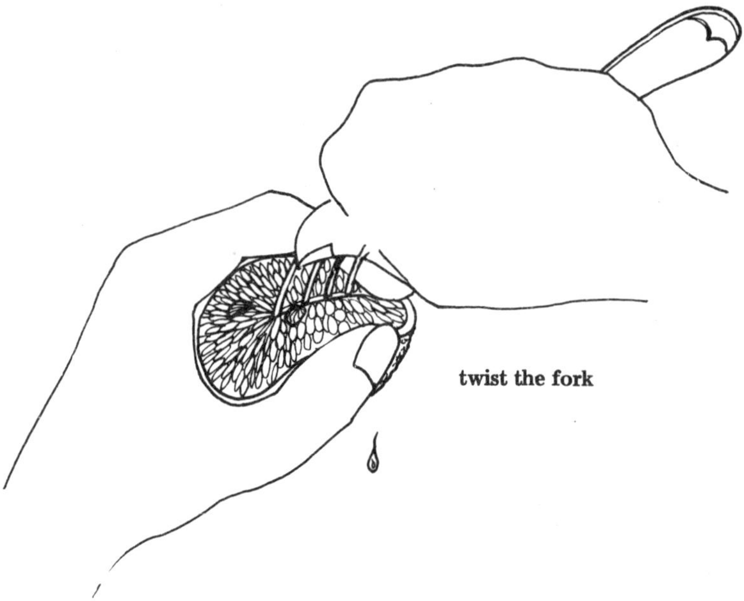

Figure 16.1 How to squeeze the juice from a lemon

It is quick and easy to squeeze the juice from a lemon using a fork as shown (figure 16.1), and it makes less washing up. Grasp the half lemon in the left hand, holding the lemon upright so that the pips remain inside. Hold a fork in the right hand and sink the fork into the lemon and twist round.

RICH VANILLA CHEESECAKE

This is made from rich Philadelphia cream cheese with a topping of soured cream and a base of spiced digestive biscuit crumbs.

125 g digestive biscuits, 50 g butter; ½ teaspoon cinnamon; ½ teaspoon nutmeg; 450 g Philadelphia cream cheese; 125 g caster sugar; 2 eggs; 1 teaspoon vanilla essence; Topping: 60 g caster sugar; 150 ml soured cream; a few drops vanilla essence.

Pre-heat the oven to regulo 6, 200 °C (400 °F). Crush the biscuits using a rolling pin, or put in the blender. Melt the butter in a saucepan, stir in the biscuits and spices. Grease the bottom and sides of a 20 cm loose-bottomed cake tin. Press this biscuit crumb mixture evenly over the base. Bake for not more than 10 minutes or until brown and crisp. Cream together the cheese and sugar in a large bowl using a wooden spoon. Add the eggs one at a time, and the vanilla essence. Beat until smooth. Pour over the biscuit crumb base and bake at regulo 5, 190 °C (375 °F) for about 40 minutes or until it is set. Remove from the oven and slip the point of a sharp knife around the edge to loosen. Allow to cool. Meanwhile whisk the sugar, soured cream and vanilla together until the sugar has dissolved. Pour it over the cheesecake (still in its tin) and allow to set. Unmould to serve.

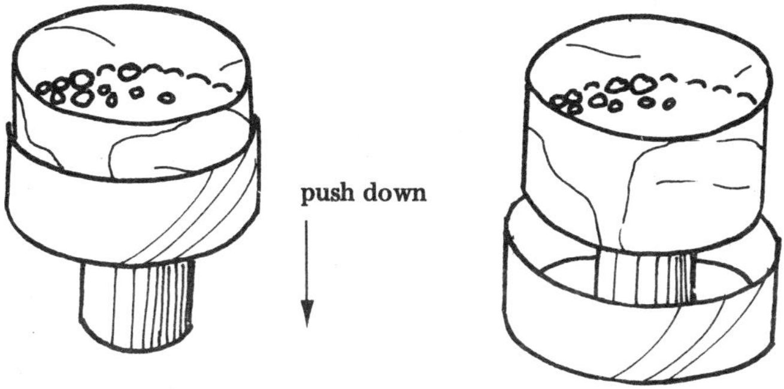

Figure 16.2 Removing a cake from a loose-bottomed cake tin

To remove a cake from a loose-bottomed tin, stand the cake on a tall can of food. Push the sides of the cake tin downwards, leaving the cake on the base standing free (figure 16.2).

17

The Appeal of Food

'Harmony, contrast and accent are the three principles of the culinary art. The art of Chinese cooking lies in the selection, blending and harmonising of texture, colour, aroma and taste . . . The Chinese feast is a study in contrast; sweets are played against salts, smoothness against crunchiness, large foods against miniature ones, hot foods against cold ones'
From *The Fine Art of Chinese Cooking*, by Dr and Mrs Lee Su Jan.

An artist's painting which has one or two predominant colours contains many others tactfully placed or used in subdued tones which help create the total impact. Without them there would be a flat monochrome effect, lacking interest and balance of hue. Likewise, the taste of food we eat is aesthetically well balanced or not according to how the taste-sensitive nerves of the tongue are brought into play. The basic tastes of food are less easy to analyse and classify than colours. Salt, sweet, sour, acid and bitter are five basic and identifiable tastes. In high-class Chinese cooking in which particular regard is paid towards the aesthetic aspects of food you will see how all these tastes are related and used for the total effect. A savoury meat dish may contain every one of these five tastes. Provided they are balanced well the taste can be sublime. Our satisfaction in taste works on the same principles as the appreciation of colour in a painting. The above quotation underlines the meaning of this.

It also applies to the presentation of food, that is, how it is decorated or garnished and how it is set off in attractive dishes with napery to match. It also applies to the way in which dishes are put together in the making of a menu.

Most people are charmed by the visual appeal of a nicely

presented dish since it excites the appetite. One's expectation of the food is in relation to this — if it has been made to look exceptionally good it must also taste exceptionally good. In the presentation is the promise of what is to come. Food must taste as good as it looks and live up to this promise. Whatever you do towards this end pays a compliment to your guests and to your cooking.

Many savoury dishes are garnished, while sweet ones are decorated. Basically it means the same. It is more common to have an edible garnish than one which cannot be eaten. This was often the case in the last century. Old-fashioned English puddings, for example, were presented alongside flowers, jellies were decorated with maidenhair fern while a blancmange might have been set on a white dish alongside a scarlet geranium.

In the home it is necessary to have quick and simple garnishes that are easily brought into effect. These are quite distinct from the composite garnishes of French *haute cuisine*, where the skills of several chefs — meat chef, sauce chef, pastry and vegetable chefs — are combined to produce one dish alone.

These sophisticated garnishes often form a substantial part of the meal itself: pastry tartlets filled with poached vegetables, artichoke hearts stuffed with *bearnaise* sauce, *foie gras* mousses, crayfish tarts in aspic, and so on, often named after special events, places or important people. These have their place in high-class restaurants, but are so time consuming for the individual as to be impracticable in the home.

In any event, a garnish is meant to enhance a dish, adding texture (for example, toasted almonds on baked trout), colour (for example, sliced tomato on a creamy sauced dish) and taste (for example, lemon wedges alongside a fish dish). Often they do all these things, and may accentuate or contrast. A garnish or decoration may at the same time be informative in telling us what a dish is composed of if this is not immediately apparent. For instance, a fish pie may be decorated with a pastry cut-out of a fish or an orange mousse may have a few telling strands of rind arranged daintily in the middle. Whatever it is, it must not be misleading. Neither must a garnish be overdone, otherwise it will both conceal and detract from the dish itself. A garnish must add something to the main dish and not take over.

Hot garnishes on hot food must be quick, otherwise the

food will get cold. For the elaborate cold buffet, however, it is possible to spend more time on decorating and garnishing such dishes as fish in aspic, savoury mousses, galantines and so on. It will also reflect the spirit of an elaborate occasion.

The choice of serving dishes and napery also sets off the style of the food and the occasion. It is not possible to have a range of these things to suit every kind of meal, but it helps if you bear the idea in mind. Country-style food looks best on thick country-style plates and dishes. Sophisticated food should be served on fine china, with silver spoons and cut glass and candelabra. A brightly checked tablecloth suits breakfast — and so on. Whatever the occasion, the food should fit the dish nicely, neither looking lost because there is not enough of it, nor overflowing with sauce or garnish. Remember also that dark foods are set off in a white dish, while a creamy sauce looks best in a brightly coloured or a dark dish.

Not every dish is improved by elaboration, however. It may be appealing in itself, either because of its simplicity or because it contains so many colours and textures that garnishing would be lost. A cheese board should be left unadorned, as should a soufflé risen high from the oven. Pizzas, salads and many rice dishes should also be left alone —they are colourful and decorative in themselves.

Devising the meal itself involves planning the juxtaposition of dishes, usually in an order. There may also be a focal point — the main dish — which will be the climax of the meal. After the meal we should finish with a sense of well-being, brought about by having a well balanced, interesting menu.

A menu should have freshness and variety of colour, and also of texture. An example of one that fails on both scores would be a white *vichyssoise* soup, followed by fish in a white sauce, ending with vanilla blancmange, which is also white. On similar lines, no food or garnish should be repeated throughout the meal. Another failure menu would be to have *quiche lorraine*, followed by baked fish *en croûte* with apple pie to end: this menu is all pastry. Another disaster would be to start with a bowl of thick soup and French bread, followed by a hearty meat and potato pie and ending with a warming treacle sponge pudding. The total menu is far too heavy, and you may not finish it before becoming too full. Try to avoid making the menu over-rich with cream, fatty or fried foods. You should try to serve something sharp with or after fatty foods. With dry foods, serve an emollient sauce. The styles of cooking should be varied between courses, so, for example, a fried food is not repeated, but is served before or after a baked or a poached dish, and so on. Try also to vary the temperatures of the courses. This not only makes it more interesting, but also means that the cook has a chance to complete some advance preparation. There should be emphasis on warm foods during winter and light meals during the summer, however. The time of year should also affect the choice of foods because fruit and vegetables in particular are at their best when in season. They are also at their cheapest. Furthermore, one's appreciation of foods in season is heightened if they are only eaten *when* in season, as distinct from being brought out at regular intervals from the deep-freeze. Strawberries go with warm sunny days, blackberries with the onset of autumn, and so on. The anticipation of it all is part of the fun of eating these foods when they first come fresh on to the markets.

There are many other considerations in devising a menu, not necessarily to do with cooking or with how well balanced the menu is. An inexperienced cook should not attempt more than he or she can cope with. However, any restrictions should in no way lessen the success or enjoyment of the meal, but the choice should take into account the capabilities of the cook. It is not a good idea to try out a new dish on important guests, either, but better to practice on family or friends, who you know will not mind if it is anything other than perfect. Allow plenty of time to eat and appreciate the meal, leaving an extended meal for the evening. Lunch times are generally restrictive and when working in the afternoon a heavy meal is out anyway.

For foreign visitors, choose to cook one of your national dishes rather than trying to make them feel at home by cooking one of theirs. For the family, keep introducing a new dish so that they have a wide variety of interest. The ultimate choice of food, however, is according to whether you or the people you are cooking for actually like it. When cooking for someone for the first time, it is a good idea to discover in advance their dislikes. Failing this, it is safe to avoid strong foods, including game and all offal, which many people cannot eat.

Bon appétit!

18

Indian Cooking — making a start

India is so vast that, with all its cultures, it is not possible here even to summarise its various cuisines. This chapter is a lead towards cooking the kind of dishes enjoyed by one family in Bombay. The family is a Parsi family who eat meat and fish dishes and, like all Parsis, exclude beef from their diet because they respect the Hindus' reverence for the cow. They eat mutton, goat and fowl and all edible parts that can be used are made into tempting dishes. The brains of sheep are gently stewed in a sauce of tomatoes, ginger and fresh coriander, while large marrow bones are stewed until the centres are soft, and given as a treat to the children to scoop the jelly, using long silver marrow spoons presented to them in much the same way as silver napkin rings are given to infants in this country. No meat in India reaches the prime quality we enjoy in Europe—there are no roasts as we know them or fillet steaks tender and rare — in fact, the meat is not even butchered into recognisable joints, but is simply chopped off the carcase according to the quantity required, and as it comes. Meat has to be stewed for a long time and slowly to make it tender — or it is tenderised by marinating in curds (that is, yoghourt) for several days, as for *tandoori* chicken, or pickled in vinegar as for *vindaloo*.

One of the most important pieces of kitchen equipment in this and many other Indian kitchens is the pressure cooker: it is used for cooking meat and lentils before being mixed with the spices frying gently alongside in a separate frying pan or *karhai*. As cooking is performed mostly on the hob, fed by bottled gas, it is understandable that they should conserve fuel by using the pressure cooker in this way. There is comparatively little use of the oven, where the pressure is not strong enough to give the high baking temperatures we are used to anyway. Using the oven is considered extravagant.

The second vital part of the kitchen is the traditional grinding stone, situated on the floor in one corner where the servant kneels and grinds the spices selected for her for the day's needs, using a kind of stone rolling pin. On adding water to the dry spices they become a wettish paste or *masala* as she works.

Merchants call at the door daily with fresh fruits, coconuts and other essentials, otherwise most of the shopping is done in a street market in the area known as Colaba, or under cover in the large and bustling Crawford market. Fish is purchased direct from the harbour early in the morning.

If there is a birthday or some other celebration in the household, the entrance and the doorways inside will be festooned with garlands of sweet-smelling jasmin and other flowers and around one's feet the floor will be decorated with delicate designs of fish, flowers and intricate geometric shapes stamped out in chalk through special perforated metal trays, bought and collected for just such occasions.

The family meet for the first formal meal of the day at lunch time, enjoying a cool lager or Scotch beforehand. Indian lager is excellent. The first dish to be served is likely to be a dry spiced fish dish, prepared with a popular fish called pomfret, eaten on its own, followed by two or three different curries and rice. (The English word curry comes from the southern Indian term *kari*, meaning a dish with a liquid sauce. A dish having a dry sauce is not a curry as such.) Should one of the curries be hot with chillies *raita* will be served (a cooling yoghourt preparation), in addition to various fresh chutneys and pickles. Fresh fruit follows, and a pudding. Typical Indian puddings are flavoured with cardamom, saffron and rosewater, and many are made from curds and semolina. However, the lady of the house might have decided to do an English or a French pudding as a change, and it is quite possible that a trifle will be served, or a soufflé, instead of a traditional *rava* or *rosgullah*. In the evening there is a meal on similar lines to lunch, perhaps including some item left over from the lunch-time menu. There is never any waste. If a full meal is not required a snack will appear which is quite likely to be scrambled eggs — Indian-style, of course — or eggs and spiced vegetables fried up on similar lines to a Spanish omelette, or a quick and simple minced meat bake.

Parsi families like going out and also entertaining, but entertaining is nearly always done in private homes, rarely in restaurants. There might be an occasional evening out to a Chinese restaurant for a change, or to a *tandoori* restaurant for *tandoori* food. They enjoy alcoholic drinks: a drinks cabinet is likely to contain Indian scotch and Indian lager and beer, also Scotch and a number of French and Italian aperitifs brought home by a friend or relative returning from a holiday or business in Europe. Indian wine is available, but is best left alone.

The spices needed for cooking the dishes in this chapter are listed below. There is one special piece of equipment essential if you are busy: a small electric coffee mill, reserved solely for grinding spices. The recipes that follow are for typical dishes cooked and served daily in a large and busy Indian household.

INGREDIENTS USED IN THE RECIPES

Aubergine A fruit used in savoury dishes. It tends to taste bitter unless it is first prepared by slicing or cubing, then sprinkled with salt and allowed to exude the brownish bitter substance; this takes about ½ hour. It is then rinsed and is ready to use.

Besan Chick-pea flour. Substitute wheat flour if not available.

Black mustard seeds They are always fried in ghee or oil before use, but have a habit of jumping right out of the pan, so keep a lid on.

Cardamom pods White, green and black. The white and

green ones are used mainly in sweet dishes and are very expensive. Buy 50 g at a time. The seeds are usually removed and ground but sometimes the black pods are simply split open and added whole. They are all very fragrant. The powder of white and green cardamoms can be added a pinch at a time to a pot of tea.

Cashew nuts The unsalted ones are available from health food shops. If they are to be ground, buy the broken ones, which are cheaper.

Chillies Red or green and very hot. The Indian ones are small and thin, while chillies available in most supermarkets are the African variety, which are larger and fat but can also be used. The pod should be split lengthways and the seeds removed. Care should subsequently be taken not to rub your eyes or nose with the fingers or they will sting badly.

Chilli powder Very hot. Cayenne pepper may be used instead.

Cloves Sometimes used whole or they can be powdered. An ingredient of the spice mix called garam masala.

Coriander A long-stemmed herb resembling flat-leaved Mediterranean parsley. Also available from Greek and Cypriot delicatessens. Fresh coriander keeps well, for up to a week if wrapped in polythene and kept at the bottom of the refrigerator. [Do not confuse with coriander seeds (dhanya).] Used to flavour sauces and for garnishing, much as we would use parsley to scatter over a dish.

Cummin seeds Called jeera. They are sometimes crushed with the back of a spoon and used whole or they can be powdered.

Curds Use plain yoghourt.

Dal The name given to split lentils, whether raw or cooked. There are many varieties, including val dal, masoor dal, toover dal, channa dal and mung dal. These can all be used in *dhansak*. Failing that, use the bright orange lentils available from supermarkets (masoor dal).

Garam masala A spice mix containing at least black peppercorns, cloves and cinnamon, but can also include cummin, cardamom and coriander seeds. It is a convenient way of adding a number of different spices to a dish.

Ghee A kind of clarified butter sold in tins. Animal ghee is very expensive, and the vegetable ghee is most commonly used by Indians in this country. Ghee melts to a beautifully clear golden liquid and although butter or oil may be used as a substitute it should not be compared. Greek delicatessens also stock ghee.

Ginger Use the fresh root ginger. It is now available in supermarkets and somewhat resembles Jerusalem artichokes in appearance. It keeps well, and should be stored uncovered in a cool place. If it becomes wrinkled, this does not matter. Scrape off the papery skin, then chop it or grate finely.

Haldi Turmeric.

Jeera Cummin.

Jaggery After the sugar cane has been boiled it is poured into tubs, in which it sets as a soft brown sweet substance called jaggery. Substitute soft brown sugar.

Methi A pungent herb, usually available in the dried form.

Rosewater A favourite ingredient in Indian sweet dishes. Fragrant. Available from large chemists. It is usually cheaper to buy in large amounts in bottles of up to 500 ml.

Saffron The pistils of a crocus. Used to be grown in Saffron Walden but now comes from the Mediterranean. The pistils should be made into a powder, then infused in a little boiling water to extract the colour and flavour. It is very fragrant. Used a lot in rice dishes and also for puddings. Tumeric is *not* a substitute. In some households, the rooms of guests would be scented with saffron for their arrival.

Turmeric Haldi. A dark yellow powder from a dried root. Used in nearly every savoury dish.

Yoghourt Curds.

LAMB KORMA

A dry spiced meat dish, cooked with curds and thickened with ground cashew nuts.

> *500 g lean boneless lamb; 275 ml curds (use plain yoghourt); 1½ level teaspoons salt; 1 onion; 1 green pepper; 2 to 4 cloves garlic; 3 cm piece root ginger; 1 small bunch fresh coriander; 5 to 6 tablespoons melted ghee; 1 teaspoon garam masala; ½ teaspoon chilli powder; 1 teaspoon turmeric; 2 to 4 tomatoes; 1 tablespoon desiccated coconut; 75 g ground cashew nuts; a little water.*

Trim the meat and cut into cubes. Place in a pan that has a well-fitting lid together with the yoghourt and salt. (It may surprise you that there is no other liquid used.) Bring to the boil, then turn down to simmer and cook for about 1 hour with a tight lid or until the meat is tender. Slice the onion, chop the green pepper, mash the garlic with salt and chop or grate the fresh root ginger. Chop the coriander—stems and leaves—and put all these prepared items with the ghee into another saucepan and fry gently, stirring occasionally with a wooden spoon. Add the dry spices. When the fat oozes from the mixture after about 10 minutes, add the cooked meat and the juices, the tomatoes, coconut and cashew nuts. Stir well and continue to cook for 15 to 20 minutes without the lid. Add a little water during this time to prevent it sticking to the pan. The final consistency should be 'dry' — there should be no runny liquid. The moist spices and vegetables should cling to the pieces of meat like a thick sauce.

An alternative to lamb is chicken, allowing double the weight because of the bone. [*Serves 4*]

In India, the term 'dry' applied to food has a slightly different meaning to that used in the United Kingdom.

DHANSAK

A well-known Parsi dish of lentils and vegetables, spiced and stewed together with lamb or chicken. It is served strewn with crisp and brown fried onions.

200 g mixed dal; enough pieces of middle neck of lamb for 4 to 6 people; water to cover; 1 level tablespoon salt; 1 small aubergine; 1 large potato; 3 skinned tomatoes; small piece red or white pumpkin if available; 1 small sweet potato if available; 4 cm piece fresh root ginger; 3 to 4 cloves garlic; 5 green or red chillies; bunch fresh coriander if available; a few mint leaves; a bunch methi bhaji or 1 tablespoon dried methi; 1 onion (first) or a few spring onions; 1 teaspoon turmeric; 6 cloves; 6 black peppercorns; 1 stick cinnamon; seeds 6 black cardemoms; 1 heaped teaspoon cummin seeds; To finish: ghee to fry; 2 large onions.

Wash the dal by covering with clean cold water, rinsing with the hands, then pouring off the water containing the dust and foreign matter. Place in a very large saucepan with the meat and cover well with water and the salt. (The amount of water is not vital since more can be added when needed. If there is too much of it later on, it can simply be reduced by cooking the dhansak without the lid.) Bring to the boil, then turn down to simmer while you prepare the remaining ingredients. Cut the aubergine into cubes, lay on a plate, sprinkle with salt and leave for 30 minutes. Rinse and add to the pan. (The salt draws away a brown liquid from the aubergine that tastes bitter.)

Peel the potato, cube and add to the pan. Chop the tomatoes. Peel the pumpkin and sweet potato if used and cube. Add all the vegetables to the pan. Scrape the skin from the ginger and either grate it or chop very finely. Peel the garlic and either chop finely or mash with salt, using the side of a knife on a wooden board. Remove the seeds from the chillies and discard. Chop the chillies. Wash the coriander and mint leaves and chop finely. Chop the methi and onion. Add all these ingredients to the pan as you prepare them. Stir in the turmeric. Place the remaining dried spices in the jar of a small electric coffee grinder and blend until reduced to a powder. Add these to the other ingredients in the pan. Allow to simmer for 2 to 3 hours or until the lentils and vegetables are reduced to a pulp of a thick creamy consistency. Meanwhile, slice the onions paper thin. Heat ½ cm of ghee in a large frying pan and when very hot fry the onions until they are dark brown and crisp. Drain on absorbent kitchen paper. Serve the dhansak in a large tureen with the onions scattered over. The onions should be so dry and crisp that they rustle; this can only be achieved by having the ghee very hot first and frying a few slices of onion at a time.

Note Using the above recipe as a basic guide, you can exclude the meat, to produce an equally attractive and tasty dish. You may wish to serve either style with pickles and chutneys, which give impact and additional flavour. (See recipe for tomato chutney, p. 178.)

NARGESI KOFTAS

Meat-balls containing hard-boiled egg. *Nargesi* meaning yellow narcissus.

> *450 g lean boneless lamb minced finely; 1 egg; 3 tablespoons chopped fresh coriander; 45 g besan or use wheat flour; 1 level teaspoon ground cummin; 1 level teaspoon salt; 6 small hard-boiled eggs; oil for deep-frying; For the sauce: 75 g ghee; 3 large onions; 4 cm piece fresh ginger root; 4 cloves garlic; 2½ teaspoons garam masala; 1 teaspoon turmeric; ½ level teaspoon chilli powder; 1 level teaspoon salt; 3 fresh or canned tomatoes, seeds removed; 150 ml water; 200 ml plain yoghourt; To serve: finely chopped fresh coriander.*

In a large bowl, beat together the meat, raw egg, coriander, besan, cummin and salt. Divide into six portions, forming each into a circle big enough to wrap around one hard-boiled egg. Completely envelop each egg and pat into a neat oval shape. Heat the oil to 190 °C (375 °F) and fry the koftas for about 3 minutes, turning them over to brown evenly on all sides. Drain on absorbent kitchen paper. Make the sauce by first melting the ghee slowly in a large frying pan. Slice the onions very finely and add to the pan. Scrape the ginger root and chop finely. Chop the garlic and add both to the pan with the onions, together with the dry spices and salt. The onions should be softened after 7 or 8 minutes. Put the tomatoes in the jar of an electric blender, together with the water, yoghourt and the onion mixture. Blend at high speed until smooth. Pour this sauce into a saucepan. Add the koftas and heat gently together. Serve in a heated dish sprinkled with the coriander. [*Serves 4 to 6*]

TOMATO CHUTNEY

Chutneys and pickles add interest and flavour to all dishes and are served separately for people to help themselves if they wish. They are particularly good with dal and rice and other dishes that have little accent of their own.

275 ml canned tomatoes; 200 ml white or brown malt vinegar; 3 cm stick cinnamon; 2½ level teaspoons salt; 175 g jaggery (use brown sugar); 8 whole cloves; 1 small onion; 4 cm piece ginger root; 2 cloves garlic; 2 red or green chillies; small bunch fresh coriander; 2 tablespoons oil; 1½ level tablespoons black mustard seeds.

Put the tomatoes in the pan with the vinegar and bring to the boil. Turn the heat down and simmer uncovered while you prepare the other items. Add the cinnamon, salt, sugar and cloves. Slice the onion very finely and add that. Scrape the skin off the ginger and either grate or chop finely, then add. Chop the garlic, the chillies and the stems and leaves of the coriander. Add them all to the pan as they are ready. Continue to cook and reduce, uncovered until the mixture becomes thick. Meanwhile in a separate pan, heat the oil. Have the lid of the pan ready to cover. Add the black mustard seeds and as they begin to jump, cover with the lid and remove from the heat. Add these and the oil to the chutney. Pour into clean warmed jars. Although in India chutneys and pickles are made to be eaten fresh this one does keep well for several months.

RAITA

A cooling preparation of curds, useful as an accompaniment to very hot dishes. It usually contains black mustard seeds, plus one or two vegetables such as cucumber or onion, cubes of potato, aubergine or coconut, banana, mint, and so on—the variations are almost endless.

1 level teaspoon black mustard seeds; 1 tablespoon oil; ½ cucumber; 200 ml plain yoghourt; ½ tablespoon finely chopped onion; salt.

Heat the mustard seeds and oil together in a pan with a lid. Withdraw from the heat when the mustard seeds begin to jump and crackle. Set aside. Peel the cucumber and slice very thinly. Mix together all the ingredients, including the oil, in a basin, with salt to taste. Chill. Serve in small dishes.

CACHUMBHAR

A simple side salad that can accompany any spiced dish.

2 tomatoes; 1 tablespoon finely chopped onion; juice half a lemon; 2 cm piece fresh ginger root; 3 hot red chillies; leaves from 8 or 9 stalks fresh coriander; salt to taste.

Cut the tomatoes into pieces and put into a bowl with the onion and lemon juice. Scrape the skin from the ginger, then either grate finely or chop. Discard the seeds from the chillies and chop. Chop or tear the coriander leaves. Put all these together with the tomatoes. Add salt to taste. Refrigerate for 1 hour before serving.

RAVA

An exotic semolina pudding, flavoured and scented with rose-water, cardamom and saffron and strewn with toasted shredded almonds.

A pinch of saffron; 4 to 5 tablespoons rosewater; 24 green or white cardamom pods; 125 g semolina; 75 g butter; 1¼ l milk; 125 g sugar; 50 g ground almonds; Decoration: grated nutmeg; 75 g whole almonds; 2 tablespoons oil; 50 g currants.

Put the saffron pistils in a small saucepan and hold over the heat for a few seconds to drive off the moisture. Allow to cool a little after which they will become really crisp, then crumble to a fine powder between the finger and thumb. Add the rosewater to the saffron, bring just to the boil then set aside to infuse for 10 minutes or so. (This draws out the colour and flavour of the saffron. Normally, however, it would be infused in plain water.) Remove the seeds from the cardamom pods and place with the semolina in the jar of a small electric grinder. Blend for a few seconds until the seeds break up. They may not go to a complete powder, however. Melt the butter in a large saucepan and blend in the semolina. Cook for a minute or two over a moderate heat without browning, stirring constantly with a wooden spoon. Remove from the heat, then add the milk a little at a time, stirring well between each addition. When all the milk is used up return it to the heat and bring to the boil, stirring constantly. Add the sugar, the rosewater mixture and ground almonds if used. Cook gently until the mixture thickens and leaves a thin trail when dribbled from the spoon. Pour into a large glass bowl. Grate the nutmeg evenly and lightly over the rava. Meanwhile, blanch the almonds and remove the skins. Cut into shreds (little sticks). Heat the oil in a frying pan and in it toss the almonds until golden brown. Remove from the heat and stir in the currants (do not fry the currants because they will burn). Serve the *rava* cold or chilled, strewn with the almonds and currants. The texture should be like soft curd cheese.

When making in advance do not cover the pudding or the moisture will make the almonds turn soft. Alternatively, add the almonds just before serving — this way they will taste better and will be crunchy. [*Serves 6*]

Index of Recipes